# BECOMING 1

Twelve Steps to Achieve

Unity, Agreement and Oneness

## HARRY & CHERYL SALEM

**2 Becoming 1**

ISBN 0-924748-72-9
UPC 88571300042-0

Printed in the United States of America
© 2006 by Salem Family Ministries
P.O. Box 701287 Tulsa, OK 74170

Milestones International Publishers
140 Danika Dr., NW
Huntsville, AL 35806
Phone: 256-830-0362
        303-503-7257
FAX: 256-830-9206
E-mail: milestonesintl@bellsouth.net
www.milestonesintl.com

**Disclaimer:** The views expressed in this book contain Harry and Cheryl's personal opinions and experiences through their lives and marriage. They express them as their opinions and views only, and share them with you from their personal lifelong experiences, from their hearts. They are only communicating what has worked for them personally, not as counselors, but as husband and wife.

# DEDICATION

This book is dedicated to both of our parents for their examples in marriage and as partners for life, as well as to Dr. Oral and Evelyn Roberts as spiritual parents, and for Dr. Roberts honoring us with the forward in this book. We would be remiss if we did not also, dedicate this book to our sons who inspired us to write this book as one of them said, "Daddy, I hope I have a marriage just like yours one day."

Harry and Cheryl Salem

# FOREWORD

In recent months Harry and Cheryl Salem have been visiting me in my home. They have come along on occasions and at times with some of their dearest ministry pastors and friends for my mentoring. Every time I am with them I am amazed at the knowledge they have acquired over the years as they have as I have told them "been giving so much to the Lord and creating and leaving a trail of the gospel across America." Their growth and maturity in the Lord is so evident in their lives and ministry as a family, but more than that, their insight and revelation about marriage and becoming one will amaze you as it has me.

I remember writing them a number of years ago (1998) when my darling with, Evelyn, (my partner in life for some 66 years who recently went home to be with the Lord) and I watched a tape of their ministry on marriage and I recall having written them and telling them that "even in our old age you help us understand each other better." I remember even then feeling the presence of God coming through the television.

I feel in my spirit their new book on marriage "2 Becoming 1" should be the book that every mother would want their son to have, and every father would want their daughter to have.

I believe in this couple as ministers of the gospel, but more than that; I believe in the calling of God on their lives. I have know them personally for over 25 years and have seen firsthand how they have faced adversity, and come through the fires of life as those three Hebrew children did without even the smell of smoke on them. They have been tried in the fire and with the leading of the Holy Spirit have brought their revelations on marriage out of the ashes for you and me to learn from.

If I were you, I would read this book from cover to cover and drink in the "good stuff" that will enrich your life.

Dr. Oral Roberts
*Founder and Chancellor Oral Roberts University*
*Founder Oral Roberts Ministries*
5.26.06

# INTRODUCTION:
# NEW BEGINNINGS

## *Cheryl*

*What would you like to receive from this book?*

If your marriage relationship is already solid, you may be looking for the next level, phase or stage of a deeper, higher relationship with your mate.

If your relationship is shaky or unsteady, you may be looking for some solidity, the Rock on which to build a firm foundation.

If your marriage relationship is lifeless, you may be looking for a miracle to breathe life back into it, or a word from God that has the power to raise the dead!

If you are not married, but in the future you would like to be happily married with a godly relationship that transcends these earthly bounds, you may be looking for the one true treasure for future relationships that you have not been able to find before.

We pray that whatever you seek, you will be able to find answers to fulfill your needs. No matter the position in which you find yourself right now, we believe God wants to take us deeper and higher, ever spiraling toward the Center of all peace and happiness, which is God Himself.

The title of this book, *2 Becoming 1,* gives some insight into the mystery, intrigue and suspense of the pages to come. Many enter into this most important relationship with visions of fairy tales, imagining pixie dust sprinkling down and, *poof!* A happy marriage! But a successful and fulfilled marriage is not made so easily; it is developed through time and discovered like a priceless treasure waiting to be found.

In marriage, just as in anything while we are here on this earth, there will be better times and worse times. However, it is not what happens to us in life that shapes our future, but rather the choices we make in the midst of what is happening to us. What do we choose? How do we respond? How do we react? Maybe the true test of life has very little to do with the circumstances or situations in which we find ourselves, but with our reactions to these changes, situations and circumstances!

The molding of two very unique and independent humans into the unfathomable and remarkable relationship called marriage is a journey. Sometimes it seems long and difficult; but it brings great reward, priceless treasure, crowns and jewels for all eternity. Most of all, this great and mysterious expedition is marked with danger, difficulty and suspense. This journey truly brings a higher level of testing and trials.

# Introduction

We all find ourselves in the midst of unpleasant life experiences at one time or another. What are our responses, reactions, words or thoughts toward these things? Are you one who gazes upward toward a solution of great reward? Or do you gaze toward the ground in lost hope, all expectation depleted?

God's best for us is to look past our present situations and circumstances toward a better way, a more fruitful choice that can cause breakthroughs in our most difficult situations. Life on this earth will never be without some challenges. For without the darker times, how would we ever be able to identify the lighter ones?

Our main goal in sharing this message is to help each reader to be able to take the higher road of discovery. It is our hope that we can help you so that during the darker times in life you will learn not to turn inward, taking what is meant to be a commitment for a lifetime and turning it into bitter arrows that wound, kill and destroy. The destruction affects not only our loved ones, but also ourselves. Bitter words can spill out of a mouth that was created to bless and to praise and to lead others to a healthy way of living. These words can become the darts used by the enemy to distract us from our ultimate destiny of discovering the wonderful treasure of unity, oneness and successful, happy relationships.

We can learn to guard our mouths and keep those spiteful, prideful whips from coming forth and striping the back of someone we dearly love. Once words are spoken they can be forgiven, but they are rarely forgotten. Restoration can come forth; but the words cannot be erased or reversed. The one whose spirit those bitter words have reached will bear the scars for the rest of life's journey.

# 2 BECOMING 1

We hope this book can help you to identify any crippling thoughts, words and ideas you may harbor toward your relationships. We desire to help you reveal within yourself the Light that illumines every hidden crevice of the heart, mind, will, soul and emotions. And we pray this book can help you to read the Map – the Word of truth – that contains all the directions and reveals the twists and turns along the way to the treasure of a godly relationship.

Much of God's truth for us is hidden away. But it was never intended to be so completely hidden from us that we cannot find it and put each nugget of treasured truth into practice each day of our lives. It is our hope that as we journey together through the depths and heights of these next eight chapters, God's Way will begin to unfold before us as a path so inviting that none can resist it!

We have written eight chapters for a reason: The number eight is often used as a biblical symbol of new beginnings. So many times in life we try to start again in the middle of a thought, a project, a relationship; yet we are still building upon the old way of doing things. We find that building upon the old only makes for a less secure future structure. God loves to give us a new beginning for every relationship. Even our vertical relationship with Him is based upon a new start! (See Isaiah 43:18-19.) It doesn't matter how many times you have failed in past relationships; God's desire for you is to have a better, more fruitful tree of life in your future relationships. He wants you to be in a healthy position, mentally and spiritually, so that your own tree can produce better, sweeter fruit without the sting and destructive power of the past constraining your future relationships.

# Introduction

In my relationship with Harry, I have had to learn to answer a very deep question: Would I rather be right or happy? Sometimes in the middle of a battle, it is worthwhile to stop and look at the situation from the other person's point of view. Get outside yourself and see how silly you look. Gain perspective by getting creative! Harry and I often say, "If you want something you've never had, you've got to do something you've never done."

We want to share some tales of adventure from our marriage. Chances are, you'll see yourself and your circumstances as you read.

*"If you want something you've never had, you've got to do something you've never done."*

When Harry and I married, we quickly discovered how different we were. I am a talker, a people person, demonstrative and very verbal with my affection. Harry was fun loving, a kidder who laughed a lot. Sounds great, right? There was just one problem: When we first met and I discovered these wonderful traits, Harry was not stressed. When he got stressed, he became like another person. Of course, under stress I did the same thing, but I didn't see it in myself!

Three months after we married, Harry was made a vice president at his job. That's when the continual strain began. He became stressed and tired, with too many people, too many problems, too many decisions, too much talking and too much listening. There was just too much everything!

Every day when he left the office, his sweet secretary would call to let me know his state of mind. This would give me a clue as to how his day had gone and how to approach him when he arrived at home. Now, I didn't learn to do this right away. Oh, no! I was not so in tune with Harry during the first few years of our marriage.

In fact, I am a take-charge type of woman who married a take-charge type of man! We managed to maneuver through the first few years without totally getting lost along the way; but the frustration and stress were, at times, very high.

We had our moments, and we discovered a few things about our relationship that were positive. But we did not uncover many real truths at first. We were just so different! From my perspective, I was the eternal optimist. The glass was always half full and there was always a silver lining.

But in my opinion, Harry had become the total opposite. As far as I could see, he was the person who always saw the glass as more than half empty. If there were a silver lining, it would end up on his bill!

With this attitude, we always seemed to have conflicts in the car. I tended to ignore those people outside my space. Since I can't change them, why bother even thinking about their actions? Harry, on the other hand, seemed to look for someone on the highway who wronged him, simply so that he would have an excuse to verbally vent.

Harry would turn into a completely different person when he got behind the wheel of the car. I dreaded getting into a vehicle with him. Most of the time he was a fun-loving husband and father. But any time someone cut him off in traffic, he would instantly become upset. Riding with Harry was an adventure for our entire family. We all sat on pins and needles, waiting for Dr. Jekyll to turn into Mr. Hyde. The children and I often prayed that we could take just one trip from beginning to end without seeing that anger, but it never happened.

My reaction to this was to try to make peace. I would say, "Honey, it's not worth it to get so upset with that person. Just let it go." All the while, I was thinking to myself, "This is so silly. Why get so upset over something you can't change?" But each time I tried to bring peace, Harry would immediately redirect his frustration from the person driving the other car to me! He would say things like, "Why do you always take their side? Why can't you stand up for me once in a while?" I didn't even know there was a side! I would think to myself, "Why did you have to say anything? Why didn't you just sit here and stare out the window until the storm passed?" It was pointless to tell myself these things, though; something inside me just couldn't leave it alone.

One particular day, I became so frustrated I knew I had to do something. I thought to myself, *"We can't live like this. Harry has got to change. I have to do something."* As I was thinking these things, the Holy Spirit whispered, "Agree with him." I immediately rebelled against the thought. I couldn't believe that God would tell me to agree with him when he was so obviously in the wrong! As I sat there trying to figure out what in this world I had just heard, the Holy Spirit whispered again, "Agree with him."

Now I was completely confused. Why should I agree with Harry? Anyone could see that Harry was clearly wrong and I was right. Further, anyone could see that if I agreed with him, it would make us both wrong! My mind raced as I tried to figure out how to avoid obeying God's voice, yet not be disobedient. Once again the Holy Spirit whispered, "Agree with him."

Finally I decided to stop fighting what I'd heard and try to make sense of it, instead. For a few moments, I felt an amazing peace. Then my "common sense" kicked in and I asked myself, "Wait. How can I agree with him when he is wrong?"

Again the words, "Agree with him," came to me. It was at that moment that it dawned on me. The mystery of all relationships revolves around these three words. Maybe if more people could learn to agree with one another, they would have better relationships.

*Maybe if more people could learn to agree with one another, they would have better relationships.*

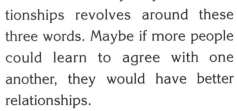

I couldn't begin to understand how this could work. Then again, nothing else I had said or done had worked. I decided to listen and obey this God-given thought that brought peace to my troubled mind. I settled it in my mind that the very next time we were in this stressful situation, no matter what, I would agree with my husband.

Not long after having this revelation, the five of us were back in the car. Once again, the familiar scenario began to unfold. A person pulled out in front of us and Harry reluctantly slowed down. I thought to myself, "If that person had just waited a few more seconds, the children and I wouldn't have to go through this again!"

Harry began a slow, angry burn. "Can you believe this person? Of course, it is probably a woman! I'll bet she's talking on her cell phone and putting on her makeup! She shouldn't even be allowed to have a driver's license!"

## Introduction

I thought to myself, "How can I possibly agree with him in this?" I heard the Holy Spirit again say, "Agree with him." I resisted, thinking, "This is not going to work. It's going to scare the children out of their minds for both of us to be acting like this!"

Then in desperation, I thought, "What do I have to lose?" I decided to stop thinking and start acting. I bit my tongue and forced myself to start agreeing with him.

I started out in a very loud voice, complete with a wild Mississippi accent, saying, "You're right, Harry. That person's an idiot! I can't believe they're driving down the road like that! Just pull up behind 'em and run 'em off the road!" My pitch was escalating more and more at this point. I was really getting into it! "You and I can jump out of the car, and I'll grab 'em and drag 'em out and hold 'em down so you can beat 'em with the tire tool!"

Harry stared at me as if I had turned into someone else right before his eyes! He stopped talking completely. He stopped everything. He turned to me and started to smile a little. Then he began to laugh, but not just a little. He belly-laughed from the depths of his soul!

Now I was really confused. Harry always wanted me to take his side, to stand up for him. Now that I was doing what he wanted, all he could do was stare at me, laughing uncontrollably. He laughed so hard that he had to pull the car over to the side of the road. The children were all laughing too. Tears began to roll down Harry's face as he laughed. Finally, as I felt the tension leave, I laughed too. I laughed the laugh of peace! I let my guard down for a few moments and our whole family laughed and laughed.

Harry told me later that one of the reasons he thought my actions were so funny was because he could almost see the local newscast flashing through his mind: *"Miss America and minister beat man with tire tool ... Film at 11 ..."*

I could not remember a time when I had seen Harry become so calm, happy and peaceful behind the wheel of a car. When the laughter subsided, I must have had a curious look on my face. He turned to me and said, "Honey, you looked so ridiculous! All I could think of was that this must be what I look like when I get so frustrated with other drivers. I actually saw myself looking totally ridiculous and I couldn't help but laugh." When we came into agreement and I was his mirrored reflection, he saw how outrageous the situation really was.

Well, this was not what I expected. I really don't know what I expected, but this sure wasn't it! However, I discovered something in those moments. Agreement with my mate had truly worked. That was an important day for our family. Now if Harry gets frustrated with other drivers the children say, "Just get out the tire tool!" and the whole atmosphere changes immediately.

That incident opened the door for us to communicate about some key issues. When we are critical, it closes the door of other people's minds. Imagine for a moment that our hearts and minds are like castles with drawbridges. We each operate our own drawbridge, deciding who or what we will allow to enter. When we are criticized the drawbridge automatically snaps shut, and no one can get in. All real communication stops. I didn't realize it at the time, but my open disapproval of Harry's words and actions had caused the drawbridge of my husband's heart and mind to slam shut.

# Introduction

When Harry grew angry in the car, I had used those moments to point out his faults. Without realizing it, I was criticizing him instead of leaving it alone or even agreeing with him. His drawbridge was immediately drawn so no one could enter.

*Honor* in the ancient Hebrew language means "to open the door." My agreement had honored my husband, which opened the door of communication between us.

Men don't like to be corrected any more than women do. Men especially dislike being corrected by their wives. In their minds, this is the first step a wife takes in becoming his mother. Women shouldn't enter into a marriage relationship in order to step into the mothering role for their husbands. Men have mothers; what they need is wives. So don't mother him. That is not a healthy position. He doesn't want you in that role, and you don't want to be there.

Now, we were married with children when this situation came up, but it was far from the first time we had to become skilled at handling our differences. From the moment we took our vows we had to learn how to handle issues we didn't agree upon.

Many people have a Hollywood mentality when it comes to marriage. In the movies, people get married and live happily ever after. In real life, there are many differences of opinion that must be worked out. A good marriage has to be negotiated. We have to compromise on our differences, with each party giving a little.

When Harry and I married, we didn't know each other very well. At the time we met, we had each decided that we would probably be single for the rest of our lives. Then, unexpectedly, we met and began to have strong feelings for each other.

# 2 BECOMING 1

We didn't take much time to date or get to know each other by spending time together before our marriage.

The very first time we sat down together to talk, Harry told me he didn't like women to wear lipstick. I did not even comment. I just kept casually talking while I walked over to the kitchen and wiped my lipstick off with a paper towel. He later told me that at that moment he thought to himself, "I'm going to marry this girl!"

I was attracted to Harry because he was strong, loyal and had a faithful character. He was very handsome, tall and well-built; but even with those wonderful outward benefits, his integrity was the charmer for me!

When Harry asked me to marry him, I agreed. I thought it would be many months before we would actually get married. But these weren't his thoughts at all. He wanted to set a date within six weeks of his proposal. When I hesitated, he gave me an ultimatum. He said that if we could not get married on that date, then the whole thing was off. But under his overly controlling manner, I understood Harry's love for me that did not want to put off our union indefinitely.

I married him, but all the while my head was screaming at my heart, "What are you doing? Have you lost your mind?" I am not a spontaneous person, so this was really an unusual thing for me to do where my future was concerned. Time has always been my friend. I wait for a long time before I jump in and do things. My life has been a series of well thought out plans. Almost everything I have ever accomplished that is of real value has been the result of much prayer, time and effort.

However, in this instance I listened to my heart and agreed to the quick date instead of listening to what I knew in my

# Introduction

head. I allowed this to happen because I truly do not like confrontation. Conflict makes me nauseous. It was easier for me to do things his way. Besides, I loved him!

Once we were married, a naive peace settled over me. I didn't foresee that our differences would cause us problems in the future. In the beginning, I went on with my life, traveling and speaking all over the country. I was usually gone three or four days every week, sometimes longer. With his responsibilities at work, Harry traveled much of the time, too.

Two months after our wedding, we met on the road for a few days' vacation. I was shocked to learn that as a result of that time, I was pregnant! Harry was stunned, but very excited. I was thankful, but once again my emotions were screaming at me! We had barely had time to get to know each other!

Harry and I had never spent any time together under any pressure. We had never had to make major decisions together. Suddenly, things changed for us. My husband became extremely overprotective, and I found this attitude incredibly difficult.

One of the traits that had first attracted me to Harry was his protectiveness. But that was before I learned that it would require me to make major changes in my life. Harry told me that I had to stop traveling so much. He told me I needed to protect my body and the baby.

My naturally independent personality flinched! Who did he think he was, trying to make these decisions for me? I did not appreciate it! I could take care of the baby and myself, thank you very much! I was intelligent and had traveled all over the world. I had done more in my 28 years than many people do in an entire lifetime. He had no idea who he had married!

# 2 BECOMING 1

All of these thoughts and emotions filled my mind. However, my desire to please and my aversion to conflict brought me into submission to my husband's will and his desire for control. I reluctantly cancelled several dates and stayed home. Inside, I was miserable. My mind raced, screamed and dug in its heels! "He will not tell me what to do! I have a mind, a will and a spirit! I am perfectly capable of making my own decisions!"

I had no idea what I had gotten myself into. On a daily basis, the visual image of jumping from the frying pan into the fire danced through my mind. The casual observer would not have seen that there was anything unusual going on in our relationship. All of my feelings were well hidden behind the mask that I had trained myself to wear. Even Harry did not know of my struggles. Since I didn't confront him, he assumed that I was happily and willingly complying with his wishes.

My new husband had a way that he thought would keep me in line. When we married, I was settled and living in Nashville. Soon after our wedding I moved my office and my life to Tulsa. Harry kept a one-way plane ticket back to Nashville in his top desk drawer.

If I gave any hint that I might not comply with his wishes, he would just pull that drawer out as if to say, "You can go back to where you came from if you won't obey me." I can't tell you how intimidated I felt when he did this to me. However, because of his upbringing, Harry was only doing what he felt was right and appropriate.

Harry was just 10 years old when his father died. For years he struggled with deep feelings of rejection and abandonment. He never let anyone know this. In fact, he never consciously realized that he had these feelings. He had a hard, tough exterior that he used to hide the hurt little boy on the inside. Harry was hard on the people around him, but he was even harder on himself.

It took me years to realize that so many of the controlling actions on both our parts were from hurts, fears and deep wounds from our pasts. All this deep-rooted pain must be revealed, dealt with and healed before truly healthy relationships can grow.

Through many years of marriage and much happiness and heartache, I have learned that agreement causes our defenses to fall down. When we are real with each other, we can accomplish much. Not only can we make real progress toward resolving our issues, but we can actually make our marriages stronger by having the courage to reveal our true selves. Doctors tell us that if we break a bone, it can become stronger than the rest of the bones in the body when it has healed. I believe this is also true with a marriage; once we break down or reveal our pain, we can become stronger ... together.

*When we are real with each other, we can accomplish much.*

We both had to change. But I think it was easier for me to change because I was seeking help and a better marriage. Harry thought we had a great marriage because he was only looking at it from his perspective. When you are on the top of the water, you never see the struggle going on beneath the water of those trying to get to the surface! And I needed to learn to be honest about my own feelings and struggles.

Until we develop a passion for reaching a new depth and level of commitment and maturity in our marriages, we may never do what it takes to change. To move forward will cost you. It may cost you your own thoughts, your desires, your past, even the person you thought you were supposed to be. You may have lost your way at some point and quit trying. You may have to begin again from where you are right now. God's desire is for us to have those new beginnings in our relationships. Let this book be a spark that sets a fire in your relationship, causing you to run toward the treasure and discover a new beginning!

### Chapter One

# CONTROLLING MAN MEETS CONTROLLING WOMAN

## *Harry*

When I met Cheryl, I had a successful career entailing many responsibilities. I had worked hard and had risen to the top – vice president! I was fulfilled in my work, which was my life. I put in long hours and reaped many rewards of my labor.

At the office I had to handle many stressful situations and make difficult decisions on a daily basis. Before I realized what was happening to me, I became a product of my environment and started turning into someone I really didn't want to be. Although it was ultimately up to me to choose how I would react to my environment, the results for my family were the same as if I'd had no say in the matter.

## 2 BECOMING 1

My Middle Eastern father taught me from a very young age that women had their place in the home and family. My dad would do anything to ensure my mother's happiness; but when it came down to it, he was the decision maker. The buck stopped with him.

I was ten years old when my father died of leukemia. At that tender age, I was told to take care of our family. My father left me with this mandate: "You will be the man of the house now. Take care of your mother and sisters. Remember what you have learned, because it has prepared you for this time and for life. Don't be a sucker for anyone. Be strong. You're a man now. Men don't cry – it is a sign of weakness. Never show emotion in public, and no one you have to deal with will be stronger than you. Never trust anyone! Confide only in your blood family. You will not embarrass me or shame our name, for you will lead and not follow. As I told you, all this will be yours. I'm sorry it came sooner than I planned, but you are ready."

From that moment, I tried to become strong like my dad wanted me to be. Although I was 10 years old, I tried to become a man and put away childish ways. Now, as an adult, I believe that becoming a man is a choice, not an age. I'll never forget going to my dad's funeral. I was told by a man there, "You are now the man of the house, so don't cry at the funeral. You are now the man of the house – act like it!"

My father, Harry Assad Salem, had a limited education and joined the U.S. Marine Corps to fight in World War II when he was barely seventeen years old. After the war, my father went into business and owned his own automobile franchise, eventually becoming president of the Automobile Dealers Association of Michigan.

## Controlling Man Meets Controlling Woman

When my father died, the Ford family ordered a Lincoln hearse to be built to carry my father to his grave. There were so many flowers that the funeral home staff lined the roadway all the way into the cemetery with bouquets. He definitely made his mark in life. I always tried to remember my father's instructions to be strong for the family. From the time I was a boy, I tried to follow his example of being the final decision maker. By the time I met Cheryl this was a very natural part of my life.

The first time I met Cheryl, a former Miss America, I did not see the self-assured, vibrant and competent woman everyone else saw. I saw a frightened little girl who needed someone to take care of her. She needed me to take care of her! I immediately saw myself as her strong knight in shining armor, her designated protector.

In one of our first conversations, I told her I didn't like women to wear lipstick. She casually got up, walked to the kitchen and wiped off her lipstick! At that moment I decided that she was the one for me. I thought she was being submissive and would make a great stay-at-home mom like my mother. I didn't realize what it had taken for my mother to rear three children without a husband; we children never felt that we were going without, or that somehow we had been dealt a bad hand. Her strength, wisdom and insight were greater than my father's. Little did I know that I was marrying someone just like my mother. Oh boy, now the journey to reality began!

When I married Cheryl, I tried to manage our relationship just as I had managed everything else in my life: with firmness and control. **It didn't take long for me to find out that there were major differences in the way a married couple communicates and the way things had always functioned in my life!**

3

In the weeks after our wedding, I discovered that Cheryl wasn't the woman I thought I had married. Although initially she had appeared to be a submissive woman, she was self-assured and confident. She had worked for years to establish herself and her career and she wasn't at all sure she wanted a man telling her what to do. I wondered where the submissive woman I thought I'd married had gone!

*We had to learn a new method of communication that benefited us both.*

When I told Cheryl to do things, she would comply with my wishes. But inside she was unyielding. She did not openly rebel, but kept her feelings inside. On the surface, I thought I had everything under control because she wasn't saying anything about how she felt. But years into our marriage, I would find that the words I had spoken to her had filled her heart with frustration and hurt. We had to learn a new method of communication that benefited us both.

In the first few weeks after we were married, I decided that Cheryl needed my business expertise. The first thing I noticed was that her office needed to be changed, so I took care of it for her via a phone call. I did not feel it was necessary to consult with my wife about the matter. We were married, after all.

I called home and told Cheryl over the phone that she was to call her office and confirm what I had just done. When she asked me why I had done so, I told her that if she had to question my decision, then maybe she should just return to Nashville. I was offended that she would question my judgment; after all, I was using my business expertise to help her. I didn't think that I had to justify my actions to my wife or to anyone else. If she was going to question me, then we were through.

I was simply doing what I had always done in business. I was correcting a problem that I had identified. Cheryl called her office and said, "I don't know what he did, but he has done it. I must submit to my husband, and even when I don't know what he's doing, I submit."

Cheryl did what I told her to do. On the outside, she submitted; but on the inside, she felt intimidated and manipulated. At the time she didn't really know how to submit with her heart and spirit; all she knew how to do was obey. She didn't realize that she needed to be willing also. For the action of obedience to be beneficial for her health and future, she needed to willingly obey. She put herself into a place of submission, but with my domineering nature and her obedient nature, what we had was more of a slave-master relationship. I gave the orders, and she complied. Neither of us was happy because the relationship we shared at that time was wrong. It was out of balance. We loved each other, but we both refused to relinquish control. Cheryl silently refused, while I verbally refused. We were at an impasse.

Since that time, we have both chipped off our rigid outer coatings. We have found the truth written of in Proverbs: "*Iron sharpeneth iron; so a man sharpeneth the countenance of his friend*" (Proverbs 27:17, KJV). We're living proof! It hasn't been easy, but it has been very rewarding. When two people marry, they each come with a different set of baggage. It's up to the individual couple to understand each other's history and navigate the course of marriage. In a marriage, it's not all about what one person wants to do; the needs of both parties must be met. **When only one person's needs are being met, the relationship is out of balance and headed for disaster.**

When we take the time to really understand who the other person is and what he or she needs, and when we try to meet those needs, we'll find that our partner will try to meet our needs too. Compromise can reap great rewards! Giving up a measure of control to your spouse can bring much freedom to your life and much peace to your entire household.

I can admit that there is a controlling side to my nature. But there is also the side of me that sees the humor in many situations we've encountered in our adventurous life together. Whatever else may be said of our marriage, it certainly hasn't been dull! I remember one disagreement we had that led to some interesting moments.

For years, I energetically searched for a place where I could find peace and quiet, a place I could call my own. It would be my personal space at home. Like most men, I needed to be able to get away from the phone, crying babies, neighbors and questions. My office was a constant flow of people with problems, and our home was a constant barrage of words, words and more words. After much searching, my car became my little world, my mini-vacation. It was my own, all mine. No one had any power there – no one but me!

This may sound strange to some people, but I just needed a place to revive myself. I don't think I'm any different from most men who want a place of refuge that they can call their own. I wanted someplace where I could be alone. I think this need to be alone is why some men work in their yard or in their garage. It's the reason others fish, hunt, build or fix things when they aren't even qualified! Have you ever put something in your living room that your husband has built in his woodshop? Perhaps visitors asked if it was something your children made at school!

When you live in a home with three phone lines constantly ringing and have children and friends coming and going, you find that there is very little time just for yourself.

First I tried mowing our lawn so I could escape the household chaos and find peace. I was proud of how great our lawn looked, and I saved a few bucks, too. Cheryl would say, "Why don't you hire someone to do that? You're stretched too thin as it is!" But this couple of hours a week was my sanctuary of solitude. Unfortunately, I injured my back and had to give it up. As a result, I lost my makeshift isolation booth.

Next, I decided to fix things, although I was limited in my fix-it skills. Once I decided to put training wheels on our son Harry's bicycle. Everything was fine for the first 15 feet. Then the wheels unexpectedly flew off, first one side and then the other. Everything was downhill from there – literally! There went Harry, crashing down the hill.

That ended my career as a mechanic. Now what could I do to find some peace? I decided to build a shed, complete with electricity. However, when I tried to run electricity to it, it turned out that being an electrician wasn't my forte, either. Another time I tried to fix the timer on the lights in the back yard. I thought the problem was a stray black wire, so I decided to fix it by attaching it in what I thought was the appropriate place. Before I knew what had happened, I found myself blown eight feet back, sitting on the air conditioner unit with black marks all over my hand. I received such a jolt from the electricity that my fillings were hot!

Next I decided to clean the gutters on our house. Thankfully, I managed to get on the roof without any mishaps. It was great! I felt like I was on top of the world – all by myself! I turned on the hose and began washing out the gutters. I didn't realize that wood shingles became slippery when wet. Yes, you guessed it! I went sliding down the roof, kicking away the ladder. I would like to think it was because of my athletic skills that I was able to save myself, but it truly was only by the grace of God that I managed to grab hold of the gutter! So there I was, dangling from the gutter, yelling frantically for Cheryl to come and help me. I waited and waited, but no one came. Finally, I had to turn loose. I just could not hold on any longer. I let go and found myself once again atop the air conditioner unit. I was banged up, but alive – and mad!

You see, Cheryl always managed to irritate me when I injured myself. It is not that she did not take care of my wounds. She did, but only after she laughed and laughed and laughed until I … well, you know. I'd say to my wife, "You laugh at my pain," and I'd storm off. "Have you no compassion?" Compassion she had, but she also had a great sense of humor!

So I was expecting this reaction and feeling slighted because no one came to help after my gutter adventure. But I picked myself up and limped into the house.

When I walked in, there was Cheryl sitting at the piano, playing and singing at the top of her lungs. The piano was Cheryl's escape. She needed an outlet, too. I just couldn't see that at the time.

"Why didn't you come and help me?" I asked in an irritated voice.

# Controlling Man Meets Controlling Woman

"Help you? I didn't know you needed me. I didn't hear you call," she explained.

"No kidding! It's no wonder you couldn't hear me with the piano, your singing, the kids making noise and the stereo playing all at once. The reason I went on the roof in the first place was to escape all this noise. I didn't realize that if I hurt myself, no one would hear me."

Cheryl could never seem to understand that I needed her to be there for me. She always seemed to operate independently from me. It was so irritating to me. I needed her and I needed her to need me.

Cheryl has her time of refreshing alone when she takes a bath. Everyone in the house knows that when the bathroom door is closed and the music is playing, Mom is relaxing in the tub. We all know that it's not the time to discuss quantum theories or ask her what's for dinner tomorrow. It is her time to break away from kids, phones, schedules, calendars and agendas. It is the time when she has no questions to answer and no problems to solve. This is her private time.

I, on the other hand, had failed to find a safe haven for myself. I had eliminated fixing bicycles, lawn work, building birdhouses, electrical work and cleaning the gutters. I wondered, "Now where can I go to have five minutes of peace?"

Then I discovered the last great escape available to me: my car. It was the perfect place to find that peace and quiet I so desperately needed. In my car, I could be gloriously alone on the way to the grocery store. (Yes, I do the grocery shopping.)

So when I spent even five or ten minutes alone in the car, it was my time. It took me ten minutes to drive to the office. During that short amount of time, I had a chance to recharge and rejuvenate my thoughts. When I drove home from work, that ten minutes alone in my car made me a better person to be with for the evening. I didn't turn on the radio or use my cell phone. No, this was my time to decompress before I got home.

I found out, though, that when you are on a public highway there are other people coming and going too. I didn't let that concern me too much because they were not in my car or my space, talking to me or asking questions or wanting answers. I was alone in my little cocoon of steel and power. My car was my castle, if only for a few minutes. But, inevitably, my beloved intruders penetrated my castle.

There were the family outings when we had dinner out or went to a movie. Sometimes the kids would ask, "Can I go to the store with you, Dad?" Other times, Cheryl would ask me to drop the kids off at school on my way to work. Or she would say, "Can I ride with you this morning so I don't have to take my car? We can talk on the way."

My castle soon became an amusement park! No peace, no quiet, the TV playing a movie or the Nintendo blaring, and voices – laughing and talking, sometimes shrieking – noise from all directions!

Our adventure would begin when the family all piled into the car. Our outing was no longer a peaceful journey in a 4,000-pound shield of refuge. Now we were a moving target on the road to exasperation. Of course, someone would always pull out in front of me. For instance, one day, a woman cut us off while darting through traffic, combing her hair, putting on lipstick and talking on her cell phone.

Now I was thinking what you must be thinking. "This woman isn't looking out for others. In fact, she isn't even cognizant that there is anyone else on the road or in this city or even on this planet." I thought to myself, "You are invading my place of refuge – or rather, my former place of refuge." That was it! My peaceful, quiet demeanor changed to that of a New York cabbie dodging the dreaded rush hour traffic.

I began to bark instructions to everyone else on the road as though I were a Drivers' Education Boot Camp Drill Sergeant conducting a Commuter Survival Course from my vehicle! I instructed everyone on how to operate a moving vehicle to obtain the desired result. It became my job to see that we all arrived safely. I had appointed myself judge and jury, and these people were all wrong. Every single one of them!

*I had appointed myself judge and jury, and these people were all wrong. Every single one of them!*

Cheryl, on the other hand, didn't see it this way. She saw me as a man possessed by some evil desire to lash out at the other drivers. She was convinced the woman who had cut us off could hear what I was saying from 250 yards away, inside a closed vehicle! To her, I was an out-of-control lunatic whose only agenda was to ruin the family outing. Then the lecture – or what I perceived as a lecture – began.

"Harry, just let it go. You don't know what they are going through right now. Maybe they have to hurry for some emergency. Honey, don't let other people upset you when you can't change them."

There isn't a man alive who likes to hear that he is wrong. When she said those things to me, all I heard was criticism,

criticism, criticism. She was like a chicken pecking on the back of my neck! I didn't hear helpful remarks or her maternal concern for our safety.

We had reached a deadlock that had turned into "He Said/She Said." Who was right and who was wrong? The battle lines were drawn. It was time to ask, "Are you ready to rumble?" And while this was taking place in our car, the offending vehicle in front of us had disappeared and had probably reached its destination.

Now we had arrived at the mall and gone into a restaurant, yet the battle still continued. And for what? The only thing I could say was that it was stupid. My search for alone time and peace had landed me smack in the middle of an all-out war.

Thankfully, my wife came up with a solution that stopped the warfare. She decided that it wasn't worth what it cost to fight with me to always be right. Both of us wanted to do things the right way. But at that point in my growth process, I truly couldn't see anyone else's side but my own. I was honestly convinced that I was right.

My wife and I have very different driving styles. When Cheryl drove the family van, everyone had to abide by her rules and go her route. She was always cautious and considerate. She's the driver who has plenty of time to make it through an intersection, but still waits for a green light to turn yellow and then red as she gently rolls to a safe, secure stop. I would always think to myself, "Cheryl, it's green, keep going! Come on! How boring!"

When I was behind the wheel, the boys would egg me on: "Step on it, Dad!" Gabrielle would squeal, "Make me stick to the seat, Daddy! Go fast, go fast!" On the other hand, Cheryl drove so slowly that joggers would pass us! In our household, I was the Driving Machine, the Hero of the Highway, the King of the Road.

## Controlling Man Meets Controlling Woman

One day we pulled out of our driveway all set for a family outing. Suddenly, an inconsiderate driver pulled out in front of us without any concern for other human beings. Although he certainly couldn't hear me, I instantly began to verbally correct him. In my mind, my family was in competition with the family in front of us. It was us against them.

As usual, Cheryl tried to bring peace to the situation. She began to think of excuses for the other driver – taking his side, it seemed to me. And because my wife is very influential with our children – they call her The Colonel – they turned on me, even though they had begged Super Dad to drive fast and have fun. Now everyone was on the side of the other driver. They were all traitors. Let the games begin!

I was sure the other driver was from the pit of Hell, and I was ready to do battle with everyone. I made a comment, then braced myself for Cheryl to take the other person's side. Suddenly, my wife turned into a completely different person. I saw something that I thought I'd never see. Now, my wife is 5'5" and weighs 120 pounds. She is a girl from a very small town in Mississippi. But right in front of my eyes, I watched as she turned into a maniac filled with road rage.

She was Linda Hamilton from the movie, *The Terminator*, with a Southern accent. She was Ellie Mae Clampett personified. She was hysterical! "You're right, Harry! That person is an idiot, a fool! Why don't you just drive up behind 'em and ram into the back of their car and shove 'em off of the road? I'll pull 'em out of the car and hold 'em down so you can beat 'em with the tire tool!!"

Now this was something! Who in the world was this woman in the car with me? I began to laugh and then the kids began to laugh. We laughed so much that I had to pull the car to the side of the road. We were all laughing so hard that tears came to our eyes.

Cheryl didn't get it. "What's so funny?" she wanted to know.

I said, "After watching you act like that, I just lost it. All of a sudden, I saw how insane I must look to you and the kids. If you looked that ridiculous to me, as an adult, what must I look like to the kids?" It was right there that I made the decision to change.

As the old Rocky and Bullwinkle cartoons would say, "The moral of the story is…" Cheryl put away her pride of always being right and simply agreed with me, even though she knew I was wrong. When she took that action, it activated an immediate change in the atmosphere of the car.

**When you agree with someone, it will make them want to change.** When she agreed with me, it was easy for me to change. In fact, our whole relationship changed. Yes, I was wrong. My motives were wrong and my outcome was wrong. Now, we are not saying that you should agree with your spouse if he is abusing you or your children or breaking the law. But most of the time we disagree over things that don't really matter. Cheryl loves to tell people now, "It is not worth it to be right." When Cheryl agreed with me, we all found a place of peace. On that day, this principle completely changed our communication with each other for the present and for the future.

## Relationship Challenge:

*When we change our minds and our thinking, outward changes will follow. Outward transformation is a result of inner change.*

### Chapter Two

# I DON'T NEED TO CHANGE –
# YOU DO!

## *Cheryl*

One evening, as Harry and I were having dinner with a couple we knew, our friend unexpectedly asked, "Do you have to work at your marriage?"

I answered a little too quickly, "Yes! I work very hard in this relationship."

Harry looked at me as if I had just grown a tail and said, "What are you saying? I don't work at our marriage? It's easy."

I replied, "Why do you think I have to work so hard at it?"

He looked stunned at my answer. But that was a moment of awakening in his life and in his mind toward our relationship.

**Often, when things appear to be effortless on the surface, the reality is that much hard work has taken place**

**behind the scenes.** Athletes, musicians, doctors and lawyers have all put much work into their endeavors. What they do does not just come naturally; they have to focus on what they do in order to become proficient in their chosen fields.

Anything that is worthwhile in life takes effort. In a marriage, we must give thought, energy and evaluation to what is working and what isn't. Many people feel that a marriage is a "soft place to fall." They feel they can relax, be themselves and just do what comes naturally.

A certain farmer worked hard to have bountiful crops each year. A friend of his gave all the credit for the crops to God. "God has truly blessed you with abundant crops," he declared. The farmer remarked, "Yes, I am thankful that God gave me good land. But I had to put a great deal of hard work into the land before it would produce. You should have seen it when God had it all to Himself!" God gave the land, but the farmer had to do the work.

In a marriage, the hard work that must take place is for a couple to transform themselves from being individuals to becoming a couple. **Most of us don't realize it, but when we marry, it changes who we are and how we look at life.** In the beginning of a marriage, each person brings his own perspective on life to the table. The goal is to forge our individual life perspectives into a united perspective while maintaining our identity and celebrating our differences.

We all understand the changes an infant must go through to reach adulthood. But by the time we marry, we feel that we are grown and set in our ways. We don't see any need to change the way we have always done things. Few individuals realize that when they get married they will have to change their perspective from that of an individual to that of a couple in order to have a successful marriage. Life is about change. We are all in a continual state of change. The evolving art of a healthy relationship plays a vital role in the success and growth of each of us individually.

One way to look at it is to recognize how a team operates. When we join a team, it is impossible for us to remain an individual. A team has to learn to work together. One person cannot "showboat." If one person on a team is only concerned with his own welfare and progress, the team cannot function efficiently. That person will soon leave the team. He will either leave on his own because he refuses to be a team player, or the coach will ask him to leave. There are many similarities in marriage. When we get married, it's the beginning of changing ourselves into team players.

When Harry and I were married, I focused a lot of my attention on his need to change. **It took me years to realize that the work I was to do in our relationship was not to look for Harry to change and become a different and better person; it was to work on changes that needed to take place in my own life.** I soon found out that the only person I could truly change was myself. Actually, the only person that I had a right to change was myself.

Changing is not easy. We generally like ourselves the way we are. We are used to who we are and we accept ourselves that way. When we choose to get married, we determine that the whole is more important than the parts. We give the marriage our time and attention. We notice what is happening in our marriage. We make a quality decision that we need to be different. It's not our mate who needs to be different, but we need to be different. It's not about pointing fingers, it's about looking in the mirror. I like to compare it to how we seek God in our relationship with Him. If we seek after riches, fame, material possessions and things, then that is what we will achieve. We may achieve riches, fame, possessions and have many things, but our relationship with Him may be lacking. If we seek after Him, then we will achieve relationship with Him, and all of the other things we desire in life will be added unto us. We'll bump into those blessings on our way to Him! (See Matthew 6:33.) It's all in where we put our focus.

In any relationship, whether it be a marriage, friendship or coworker relationship, each individual part may need to make adjustments to begin to work as a whole. When we learn to work as a couple, it takes more effort to come together because our perspective is different from that of our mate. The compromise and effort is worth it in our journey to become one with our mate.

I have noticed that when I do speaking engagements and open up the floor for questions, many people ask questions that relate to them individually. There is a strong need for them to feel safe and secure as individuals. Their focus is not always on meeting the other person's needs, even though the questions are often veiled. Here are some of the questions I am asked by women:

"How can I go along with my husband when he is wrong?"

"How can I get across to my mate that my needs are not being met?"

"What can I do when I communicate on one level and my partner communicates on another level?"

## I Don't Need to Change – You Do!

"How can I forget the hurtful words that have been said to me over the years?"

"How can I forget the memories of the bad years without regrets that affect my present state of mind?"

"Why is it that the very things that attracted me in the beginning are the things that upset me the most now?"

"What am I to do when I believe in tithing and I want to tithe and my husband does not?"

Men have their own questions:

"Why must she feel like I need to know every detail of every situation?"

"Why does she always have to take the other side of every situation?"

"Why does she always point out the opposite view point from the one that I am taking?"

"How can I be the leader, the head of the home, when she is already sitting in that seat?"

Both men and women may be thinking thoughts like these:

"What happened to the romance in our lives?"

"What happened to the spontaneity?"

"Where do we go from here?"

"Is there any road to fulfillment and happiness from this awful place we have found in our marriage?"

"Why am I always so angry and frustrated with my mate?"

"How did our relationship get to this point and can we salvage it from here?"

Some of these questions are painful for the person asking them because they are suffering and truly do not know what to do. However, much of the pain they feel comes from resistance to change in their relationship. They want to do things their own way in a marriage. When we try to operate a marriage like we do our own individual lives, it can cause us much pain.

*When we try to operate a marriage like we do our own individual lives, it can cause us much pain.*

Relationships are difficult at any level because the bottom line in all relationships is that we must actively put someone else's needs and desires ahead of our own. Some people are truly better off staying single if they are not going to get over themselves! We will have the greatest peace in our lives when we learn to die to ourselves and live beyond the needs of our own flesh. If we can do that, we will soar to a new level in all our relationships. The union of marriage is worth far more than the sum of its parts.

Consider the business world. When downsizing first began, many companies merged to save money. Employees of both companies to be merged had to learn to adapt to new ways of doing things, even though they didn't particularly like it. Later, many of these employees found that the new ways of doing things actually worked better. The company was better, stronger, more efficient and benefited the parties involved in a greater way than before. Just like the marriage relationship, the new company, which was the end result, was worth more than the sum of its parts!

Change is never easy. It is like becoming a new creation in Christ. That old, individual person passes away. This does not mean we have to give up being an individual. It is much like when a child is first brought into a home. When the new baby arrives, he changes everyone around him. Most of us do not consider this a bad thing. We are mothers or fathers and we have to sacrifice our needs and wants to meet those of a new baby. Even so, when we enter a marriage, we must meet our mate's needs and wants as well as our own.

Change can be a very emotional process for us. We have invested most of our lives in becoming who we are and in meeting our own needs first. Change has to come from the inside out. Many times we try to act as though we have changed on the outside, but on the inside our inner child is screaming to be heard. There is a saying, "A man convinced against his will is of the same opinion still." We must be truly convinced in our hearts that this is the way we want and need to live in our marriage.

When we do not embrace and accept the changes that will be necessary in our marriage or the consideration we must now give to our spouse, we will be severely disappointed. There is no way to pretend that we accept certain things in a marriage without the deep commitment to do so. Ninety-five percent of communication is nonverbal, and those cues will always give us away. There have been times when I've been very angry about something that happened. However, instead of discussing it with my husband or just living with it, I've been known to slam the cupboard doors while fixing dinner, just to prove a point! All the while, my lips would be smiling and I might be sweetly saying, "Honey," "Sweetie," "Baby." Actions always speak louder than words.

When we change from being a child into being an adult, most of us are not sorry that we are no longer children. We know that we cannot be a child forever. We look forward to becoming someone different than we were. It's the same when we get married. When we change from living a single life to living a married life there are many changes that must be made.

Change is growth. If there isn't any growth, there is only stagnation. When water is stagnant, it produces only one thing — death. We should always strive and look forward to changes in our lives. We must not be stagnant in who we are, or in any of our relationships. Our lives must be growing and producing life through us, for the sake of others and for ourselves!

When we change our minds and our thinking, outward changes will follow. Outward transformation is a result of inner change.

In order to have a healthy marriage, each partner must be at peace with themselves. We cannot have a healthy relationship until we can learn to love ourselves. When we look in the mirror, do we love the person we see? Are we happy with that person? If not, we must change those things that can be changed and learn to embrace those things that cannot be changed.

When a man and a woman merge into a marriage, they both bring their own set of baggage. The challenge with this is that each person's perspective is colored by his own personal experiences prior to marriage. For instance, the way a person communicates, what certain actions mean to him, and his reactions to certain actions can create an atmosphere of confusion. It can almost seem as though one person is speaking another language that their spouse does not understand. If one spouse has had a difficult life, their language can be very complicated to understand, particularly when that spouse has chosen not to share their history. When this happens, it can be like walking through a minefield. We are afraid that we may step on a trigger that will cause the situation to explode.

Sometimes people enter a marriage with deep wounds and internalized hurts. It's difficult to have a healthy relationship with such a person. Our advice to single people is, "Don't marry a project!" You cannot count on people changing. Any change a person may experience is totally and completely up to him or her. No one can help other people to want to change or force them to change.

If you are already married and you recognize that you are married to a project, our advice is, "Dig in and see this through! It will not be easy, but it can be worth it. Surviving and overcoming has great rewards. Don't give up, don't quit!" Surviving can become thriving with time and effort.

When people who have deep hurts in their lives marry, they often relax and allow who they really are to be seen. Then the spouse no longer sees the person he thought he'd wed. Unfortunately, such people are not motivated to change because they have already achieved the goal of getting married. Difficult people do not become better when they have already achieved their goals. Sometimes marriage can even make the situation worse.

# 2 BECOMING 1

Many hurt and angry people can be very charismatic. They sweep us off our feet. This is why it is important to not make life-long decisions based on emotion. Emotions enable us to enjoy a sunset, to express laughter, to cry at a sad movie. But emotions do not replace our brains and should not be made responsible for decisions that will affect our entire lives.

When we are considering marrying someone, it is important that we get to know each other. Harry and I did not know each other for very long before we married. Some of the things that we experienced could have been avoided if we had known each other better before we married.

A longer courtship can help to reveal the true nature of the person we want to marry. People often mask who they really are, especially if they have had traumatic past lives. Masking emotions and responses is a defense mechanism. If we wait before we jump into marriage, we can better learn what makes the other person happy, how they handle disappointments, how they treat their families, what makes them angry, what their values are and how they spend money, among other things. There are many things we need to know about that other person before we say, "I do." Physical attraction is not enough!

In choosing our mate, we need to know the answers to some important questions.

How does he deal with stressful situations?

How does she respond when she doesn't get her way?

How does he respond when you don't agree with him?

How does she act toward her parents and friends?

When out of earshot of supposedly close people, is he affirming or undermining of others?

Is she a chameleon, a people-pleaser?

Does he speak what he really feels, or does he just say to others what he thinks they want to hear?

Many people make great first impressions. These impressions may last until challenged by a situation, circumstance or stressful event. In your relationships you need to take the time to truly know more than one dimension of the person you are thinking seriously about.

*Many battles we fight in life are not against others, but against ourselves.*

We all have personal weaknesses that we must overcome. Many battles we fight in life are not against others, but against ourselves. We have to learn to overcome our own weaknesses. Often, these weaknesses come to the surface when least expected. The person experiencing the emotions is

often surprised at his own feelings. What happens is that when we are confronted with another person wanting to do things his way, it makes us think about what is really important to us.

Time reveals much about ourselves and about others. In a longer courtship, we can also see how our own interests and lifestyles mesh. Not many people would think of stepping into a business deal without thoroughly exploring it. We should do no less when considering marriage.

One couple we know of made an agreement before they married, that if something was important to one person then it was important to the other. Each person agreed to listen even when it wasn't very interesting to him or her. One of the greatest things we can do for our mate is to really listen. This couple also agreed never to criticize, condemn or complain.

These are easy things to agree upon when you are not facing them. But when difficult situations actually arise, sticking to our promises often means putting down what our flesh wants to say or do. This is always good for us. It teaches us to communicate and to think of others before we satisfy our own desires.

## Relationship Challenge:

*Learn to celebrate your differences instead of just tolerating them.*

## Chapter Three

# HE SAID...

~

## Harry

**M**en are definitely not male versions of their wives! We are not only physically different from each other, but our whole outlook on life often conflicts. When husbands and wives don't understand these differences, it causes needless friction in a marriage. It's as though we husbands are speaking Spanish and our wives are speaking Chinese – and there's no interpreter! We simply cannot understand the reasoning behind our spouse's actions. Learning to speak each other's language is one of the most important challenges we face as married couples. When this is accomplished, or at least when both parties involved give it an honest effort, there is the potential for much less strife and much more harmony in the household.

# 2 BECOMING 1

God created men to be different from women in ways that were designed to protect our wives and enhance our relationships. But it is often hard to bring our two worlds together. As males, our viewpoint, our understanding of how we should act in certain circumstances and what various things mean, comes from the fact that we have been raised and adapted into society as men. Obviously, this process is completely different from the one our wives experienced. Our wives are feminine. Praise God for it!

It seems so simple, so basic, perhaps; but learning this one simple thing can make or break a relationship. Men, our wives are not like us, and that's a good thing. They have different actions and reactions. **The challenge comes in learning to celebrate our differences instead of merely tolerating them.**

I believe men to be very logical in their approach to life. As a man, I'm expected to be level-headed in business and in society in general. But in my marriage, I have had to learn to live with the illogical woman God gave me. This takes a lot of negotiation because our instincts and viewpoints are often miles apart.

Cheryl believes that God is, in some ways, illogical. She has a point. Do the things God speaks to your heart always make perfect, logical sense? Hmm... But I believe that He is also very logical. When we read in the beginning chapters of Genesis about how God created the heavens and the earth, we find that He created with order, not chaos, and with logic, not impulse. So we can agree that God is both logical and illogical. It stands to reason that when a man and woman come together as one in marriage, they represent these two different sides of God's personality.

The challenge for a husband and wife comes in learning to understand and live with the differences in our mates. Just because a man or woman "joins our team" does not mean that he or she will change in the area of attitudes about life. The husband will always see things from a man's perspective and the wife will always see things from a woman's perspective. We have to learn to be one while still being uniquely male and female.

*The challenge for a husband and wife comes in learning to understand and live with the differences in our mates.*

For instance, Cheryl's viewpoint and pattern of communication are not like mine. She often seems to me to be illogical in the way she processes facts. Sometimes when I ask her a question she wanders off the subject into things I consider to be unimportant. This does not make me right and Cheryl wrong, or vice versa. I'm just stating the facts of our communication dynamic.

In the beginning it was difficult for me to separate the facts from the wordy explanations my wife gave me. I couldn't understand why she didn't communicate the way I did. I wanted the headlines, not the fine print! To my wife, it's the details that are important. From my perspective, just tell me the problem and I'll fix it. The details will come out in the wash. What I needed to realize was that my wife was not created to be just like me. She had years of conditioning that made her process information the way she did. That did not make her wrong, just different from me.

When we were first married, we didn't recognize the importance of our differences. We could not see any need for the other's point of view. We only saw it as "the opposite of my own," and this caused us to come into conflict on many occasions! I remember one situation we encountered that really spotlighted the differences in how we view things. The incident occurred when we flew from Tulsa to Dallas to host a television program.

We were supposed to go on that night at seven o'clock, live, on a national television program. I had given us plenty of flight time to arrive in Dallas ahead of the broadcast, but circumstances beyond my control definitely threw a wrench in my well-laid plans. Of course, this point is debatable since I was not a detail-oriented person. (Now that I think of it, perhaps I didn't even make the flight arrangements. Maybe Cheryl took care of it!)

We were perfectly content with our flight. We arrived safely in Dallas and we were taxiing to the gate when the pilot made an announcement: "There is a thunderstorm in the Dallas/Fort Worth area and the ramp is closed, so we're going to park here on the runway and wait for the storm to pass us by."

I thought to myself, "We're so close to the gate! Why in the world would they leave us out here?" There was not a drop of rain anywhere. Now we were stuck sitting on the airplane ramp and we couldn't do a thing about it! I could feel the clock ticking away while we sat there, stranded.

We were on a commuter airplane with about 40 people on board. We were in seats 1A and 1B, with the other passengers seated behind us. In my logical mind, I was sure we were going to be late.

I thought to myself, "Where is the rain? I don't see one drop of rain falling. There's no lightning, no storm clouds, nothing. Why in the world do we have to sit here? Just pull us over to the gate and we'll go about our business." There was not one bit of logic to the situation. The more I thought about it, the more agitated I got. I started to raise my voice so the attendants could hear my displeasure.

"Why would they close the ramp? This makes absolutely no sense! There's not a drop of rain, no storm, no thunder clouds. If they just drive us over to the gate we can get off this airplane right now!"

Cheryl tried to comfort me. "Harry, Matthew 18:19 says, *'Again I say unto you, That if two of you shall agree on earth as touching any thing that they shall ask, it shall be done for them of my Father which is in heaven.'* So just hold my hand and agree with me that we'll be able to get off this airplane in plenty of time."

Cheryl was not one bit upset. In fact, she just sat there quietly reading her Bible while I stressed out! Unable to avoid my obvious anxiety she said, "Honey, just agree with me, in Jesus' name, that this storm will pass and we will be able to get off this airplane with no problem. Just agree with me, right now."

"I don't want to hold your hand. I don't need to pray. I can see the gate. I need to get off this airplane."

Cheryl was still gently persistent. "We just need to pray and agree."

"I agree that there's someone in the tower who doesn't have a clue as to what they are doing!" My agitation did not help the situation. An hour went by.

"We're going to miss the TV broadcast! Cheryl, pick up the phone and call the man at the studio and tell them we're going to be late. It's six o'clock and the show goes up live at seven o'clock. We are the hosts. We need to be there right now. You had better call the man!"

Still sitting there calmly with her Bible in her lap, Cheryl made a totally bizarre statement. "Harry, I'm not interested in the time. God can stop time if He needs to."

"Time cannot be stopped," I shot back.

In the meantime, the clock continued ticking. Six fifteen. Six twenty. Six thirty.

"Cheryl, call the man!" It didn't even occur to me to call him, because she had more practice talking on the phone.

By this time, I was sure the airline was plotting against us. It was about 6:45. I was at my wits' end trying to get Cheryl to call the studio to let them know we were not going to make it when the pilot made a second announcement: "They've cleared the ramp and we can now proceed to the gate." I can't tell you how relieved I was.

We were seated, if you'll recall, at the very front of the plane. However – just to annoy me, I was sure – the plane was going to unload from the back. This made Cheryl and me, now seated in the very last row, the final passengers to exit the plane!

Our plane was filled with women going to a makeup convention. They all seemed happy and illogical, just like my wife. This only frustrated me more. How can they be so happy when they have been just as inconvenienced as we have been? As we stood up to make our way down the aisle, a man in the back of the airplane stood up and said in a loud voice, "Make a hole! Let this man and his wife through. He has driven her nuts." Now, Cheryl had been quietly praying, so the other passengers probably thought she was a babbling idiot – slowly being driven crazy by her husband!

# He Said...

Everyone stepped aside so we could get through. This was a blessing! If that man hadn't helped us we would have had to wait for all the ladies to get their bags and purses. There's no telling how long that process would have taken! When we finally exited the plane, we spotted the driver the studio had sent, patiently holding a sign for us.

"We're the Salems and we're late," I apologized.

He said, "No problem. I'll get you there in time."

Cheryl said, "Finally I have someone to agree with me!" She sat back and relaxed while I continued to fret. By this time, the rain was coming down in sheets.

Then, out of the blue, Cheryl offered to help the driver by telling him about a shortcut she knew. I shouted at her, "This guy's a professional driver and you're going to give him directions?" I was coming unglued at the seams by now!

As I stewed and doubted and listened to Cheryl offer shortcuts while still miles ahead of the exit, a major pet peeve of mine flashed through my mind. Cheryl's contribution to navigating when I drove was to sweetly say as we whizzed past a certain exit, "That was your exit." Yet here she was helping a total stranger! I just knew that everyone was against me, nothing was going right, the show was going to bomb and we were never going to be asked back. My misery knew no end at that moment!

We finally pulled up to the studio. My watch said five minutes past seven. I was frantic. The door was flung open. A lady with a headset microphone grabbed me and told me to put on this little microphone.

I apologized. "I'm so sorry that my wife didn't call you about our being late. I told her to call you. I assume you had to run a rerun because we were not here for the opening."

She didn't skip a beat. "Just get on the set." I continued to explain, "I can't believe we missed the opening of the show. I can't believe we came all this way, just to be five minutes too late."

She shoved me toward the set and I heard the music roll at the top of the program. I looked at my watch – 7:05. I continued to the set, sat down in my place, and looked up at the clock on the wall of the set. It said 7:00...right on time.

*While men are like filing cabinets, women seem to be more like computers.*

I was stumped! I wondered to myself, "How could this be?"

What I didn't remember was that I had set my watch five minutes fast that morning. Cheryl couldn't resist: "I told you God would hold the time!"

As illogical as it sounds, God did hold the time...on live TV.

My mind is like a filing cabinet. At work, I always prioritize my projects. By prioritizing the tasks that need to be done immediately and setting aside those that could be done later, I am able to accomplish a great deal. Using this process frees my mind to focus on the task at hand. When it is time for me to deal with a situation, I can just pull it out of the file cabinet, study it and decide what I'm going to do. This always irritates Cheryl, who deals with things right away. She often takes care of many tasks of different levels of priority all at once!

While men are like filing cabinets, women seem to be more like computers. They lay hold of a problem, a situation, a circumstance or something that's coming up, and they begin to deal with it right away. They think about it, they take notes, they make lists. They begin to do all the little things that might be necessary just in case something unforeseen arises. Women like the details of life. Men are not like that. If a situation comes up that can be taken care of later on, we file it away. When the appropriate time comes to deal with it, we just pull it out of the file cabinet. Problem solved.

Early in our marriage, not only would Cheryl process things like a computer, but it seemed like her timing was always off when she presented me with a problem. She often messed up my sleep time by talking to me at 10:00 at night about something that I had filed away. I would be lying there, resting, relaxing, trying to unwind. I had gotten out of my suit and tie and I was in bed, enjoying my Oreos and milk. My pillow was all fluffy, and I was at peace with the world. Then Cheryl would slide into bed and drop a bomb like, "Harry, I need to tell you what happened today."

All of a sudden, my milk would turn warm. My pillow was no longer fluffy. My cookies were soggy. And I had to deal with something that had happened that day. This wouldn't have been a problem if I didn't have a Mr. Fix-It approach to problem solving; but because I'm a fixer, I would start thinking about the situation. My mind would begin to roll. "I have to fix this! I have to solve this now!" Unfortunately, there was nothing I could do about the problem at ten o'clock at night. But by now my mind would refuse to stop. To make matters worse, once Cheryl had handed the problem off to me, she would yawn, turn over, get nice and comfy, and be ready for sleep! I, on the other hand, would be wide awake for the night.

I would snap at my wife, "Why didn't you bring this up when I got home?"

"You weren't talking when you got home. I had to wait until you had your nap. Then you were watching your TV shows and didn't want to be interrupted."

I would counter, "All right, then why didn't you call me at work?" Cheryl would give me her reasons. But that was it, the mouse was on the spinning wheel, running in earnest, and getting nowhere fast.

At such times we both felt every shred of communication slipping away, and we were both upset. Cheryl started to feel frustrated, as though she couldn't do anything right. She told me that she felt like the "appropriate time" was a moving target that was almost impossible to hit.

Through the years, Cheryl has learned never to discuss things with me before going to bed unless it's something that has the potential to ruin both our lives. Conversely, I have had to learn to live with a female computer. Computers never forget anything.

I remember one anniversary when I brought flowers home to Cheryl. It was late so I stopped at Wal-Mart and picked up a $5 bouquet.

"I'm sorry I'm late," I said apologetically. "But I had a problem at work. I did think of you, though, and bought this special bouquet of flowers."

At that point, I could hear the RAM memory making whirring noises in her head.

"Don't you remember, seven years ago on our anniversary you brought these shaggy old Wal-Mart flowers to me that you purchased on the night of our anniversary?"

# He Said...

Men, don't ever think you're going to pull anything over on a woman. They never forget a thing.

Cheryl says there are two buttons women need to use a lot more, the delete button and the escape button. She says women need to get rid of things and not constantly pull them back up, but it's hard for them to not remember. It's part of how they're made.

On another anniversary, I came into the house with a beautiful arrangement of flowers that I was sure would please Cheryl. I was so proud of myself and I was thinking that I had done something terrific this time for our anniversary. Cheryl would be so pleased. I was "The Man!" I had this gorgeous arrangement of flowers for her ... flowers, on time, huge, beautiful. Surely, she could find no fault with that! What I didn't know was that my secretary had called Cheryl before I got home and had mentioned that a pastor and his wife had sent these flowers to the office for our anniversary. I had just taken the card off and was going to present them to her from me! All I got was "The Look," and it was confession tme!

A big key to a man's self-worth is how well he feels he is doing at work. For years, I was steadfastly focused on being a good economic provider for my family. I had strong expectations for myself that I would provide well for Cheryl and the children, just as God intended. But I went overboard and had to reassess my life when I became a workaholic.

I had such an intense drive to be a good provider that I often worked excessive hours, missing quality time with my children. At one time I was working so hard that I began to have symptoms of heart problems. My hair was turning gray and falling out. I was driven to do a good job. I had begun to take on the responsibility for everything I touched. I thought that if anything failed, it was all my fault. I took the whole weight of my job and carried it on my shoulders.

Many men become obsessed with being good providers. When that happens, often it's not just the money that they provide for their family's welfare that is the issue, but that dollar sign that keeps score of how successful they are as men. One of the first questions men ask each other when they meet is, "What do you do for a living?" Men are evaluated by what they do and how well they do it. Because this is the way our society functions, it is very easy for a man to become out of balance in his thinking when it comes to providing for his family.

The result is that many men become workaholics, trying to prove themselves to their families and to society at large. Families are left to fend for themselves while the father is working too many hours. God meant for a man to provide for his family, and He also definitely intended that a man be a vital part of the family unit, not just working all the time. The man is not only a part of the family, he is to be the head of the family. Yet how can a father be the head of the family if he is never a part of it?

Today, many men also have to face the fact that women often surpass them in the workplace. Most men have adapted to these conditions at work, but it can totally undermine a man if an insensitive wife makes a careless remark about women who are doing better than he is financially. It also affects him negatively if she complains that he is not providing well enough for the family or that the things he provides don't mean anything to her.

# He Said...

When I married Cheryl, she made more money than I, she had a nicer car and she was prettier! Why should I be angry at that? And they call us stupid males!

Most wives don't realize it, but many men feel that our manhood must always be defended in every situation that we face, even if it doesn't make sense to anyone around us at the time. This is because of the way we were conditioned. Women have no idea how fragile a man's ego is on this subject. Harsh or inconsiderate words can cause a deep division between a man and a woman.

*Men are also different from women in that we are very visually oriented.*

Men are also different from women in that we are very visually oriented. This is just the way we're wired. It's important to us that our wives look good. We may not say anything negative about it, but we don't appreciate seeing our wife with rollers in her hair and wearing sweats day in and day out.

When our wives go to work, we know they get up an hour earlier than we do to prepare their outward appearance for their day at the office. They look good when they leave for work. We see them leave the house looking great.

Then, when they come home at six o'clock at night and they throw on that nasty old robe and those ugly yellow slippers they've had since college we look at them and think, "That sure doesn't do anything for me. She must care more about what the world thinks of her than what I think. She just gives me the leftovers."

Whether we like it or not, we must accept that society judges us by our appearance. A nice-looking, well-dressed man or a nice-looking, stylish woman must be better off than those who do not care for their appearance. Women, keep in mind that I didn't say "glamorous," I said "nice-looking." As far as appearance goes, we all just work with what we have! That's the best we can do. I am not suggesting that men should pursue "trophy wives" and that women must all look like movie stars. I am saying that I appreciate my wife's efforts when she takes good care of her appearance. It means more than she knows, because I know that often she is tired or worn out from her day, and when she makes that effort, especially when she is not even planning to go anywhere special, I know she has done it for me! I try to do the same for her. It's a two-way street and a little effort can reap major rewards!

My wife says while ministering in church services to ladies that it only takes five minutes to let your husband know you care about him. She tells the ladies, brush your hair and put on a clean blouse that doesn't have baby spit up on the shoulder. Cheryl works at doing these things for me in our home. She puts forth a little effort in this area for me because she knows it will please me.

Men, we are not off the hook. The same applies to us. Husbands should also take care of themselves. Some men come home and throw on gray sweatpants and an old football jersey from 25 years ago and strut around with their bellies hanging out. Listen, that's not appealing. Men, groom yourselves! A woman may not be turned on by sight or smell, but she can sure be turned off by it!

I married Cheryl for who she is inside, not for her Miss America title. Titles and appearances change, but who a person is inside will remain. That being said, I probably would not have approached her if her appearance was not visually appealing and interesting. Appearance is important to a man. Most men are visual learners. Speaking on behalf of all men, we enjoy the sight of our wives doing their best to look good for us!

When men and women do not take care of themselves and their appearance, they send a strong, silent message to their mates. "I don't need to make an effort in my appearance because I really don't care what you think." Whether intentional or unintentional, this message comes through loud and clear. As I said before, a little effort on both parts can reap huge benefits. Try it, you might like it!

Cheryl is a successful, confident woman. I think the reason she married me was that I didn't see her as Miss America, I saw her as a little girl from Choctaw County, Mississippi. I saw what no one else was even looking for. I saw her heart, and it was fragile. I saw her vulnerability, her fears, her insecurities, and then I saw her beauty. I think that's why she appreciated me and what I had to offer.

When I met Cheryl, she certainly was not lacking in charm. She'd look up at me with those big, blue eyes and ... forget about it! I never had a chance! She can win anyone over! Social graces are qualities a man appreciates in his mate. Maybe that's because many of us guys are deficient in that area. For instance, it pleases a man when his wife is friendly and considerate to the people we work with. A wife who is careless about what comes out of her mouth or what other people might think can cause friction in a marriage.

A sharp-mouthed woman causes problems wherever she goes. Proverbs 27:15 says, *"A quarrelsome wife is like a constant dripping on a rainy day"* (NIV). On the other hand, when a woman speaks with kind and pleasant words, it can bring an atmosphere of peace and love into the household. Proverbs 31:26 says, *"When she speaks she has something worth-while to say, and she always says it kindly"* (Message). The New King James Version says, *"She opens her mouth with wisdom, and on her tongue is the law of kindness."* Cheryl has always tried to do well in this area. Everyone loves my wife and she always looks good. She is pleasant to be near and she's warm to people, even those she does not know well. She is an openly kind person and she makes me proud.

Too numerous to name are the ongoing differences between the sexes! Women are deeply emotional. In the work-place, seldom is there an issue over how a man feels about something. His conclusions come from the facts. If he were to become emotional about situations that arise in the office, it would hinder the work process. A man doesn't usually respond from his emotional side as a woman does.

Men are also very physical creatures, as opposed to most women, who will avoid a physical confrontation at all costs. Men are more likely to think of punching something when they are angry. Women don't generally think this way. In sports, we are much more likely to become physically aggressive. Typically, women do not like to become physical-ly forceful. It's just not part of their nature. God, through the chemical and hormonal makeup of the male and female, has decided this for us.

It is not my intention to step on anyone's toes with my observations. I am simply taking a page from history in not-ing that the ancient men were the food gatherers, often hunt-ing or fishing to bring home food for their families. God made men strong; active, physical creatures to protect the family and to be strong for them. He gave women a different type of strength, a strength that most men just don't possess. It is more a strength of understanding, flexibility, trust and patience. The greatest strength a woman has is in her choice to submit...to willingly go under the mission of a godly relationship and home.

Generally speaking, many men have short fuses. Things can make them angry very quickly. When men are under stress, they can become physically aggressive. This is not acceptable on any level. In fact, today there are more men abusing their wives than ever before. There is never a reason for a man to become physically threatening with his wife. Abuse of any kind is wrong and has no place in any relationship.

*Time is our friend. Use it wisely*

Women need to understand that men can have a meltdown when their spouses are prone to "problem dumping" as soon as the man comes home from work. Women should try to understand that there is a right time and a wrong time to tell their husbands stressful things. When a man walks through the door after having had a tough day and his wife starts unloading the day all over him, he's either going to go up like a Roman candle or slam himself shut emotionally. Give him a cooling off period. Timing is vital in all communication.

Ecclesiastes 3:1 says, *"To every thing there is a season..."* Time is our friend. Use it wisely.

If you recognize that your mate is stressed or angry, back off and give him space. Men and women both should strive to be sensitive enough to perceive when it's a bad time for a particular conversation. Why push a "reaction button" when, if you wait, you can get a much better response?

I learned how emotional my wife could be shortly after we were married. I came home one day and Cheryl was sitting in the middle of the floor, crying. I didn't have any idea what was going on. "What's wrong?" I inquired.

"I'm sad," she said, and continued weeping.

I came home another day and she was crying. I was sure I knew what was going on, so I asked, "Are you sad?"

"No, I'm happy."

Yet another day, I came home and found her in tears again. I was sure I understood by that time that she was either sad or happy. So I ventured, "Are you sad or happy?"

"I don't know why I'm crying!" she sobbed.

I give up!

Cheryl says that crying is her way of detoxifying her emotions so she doesn't keep them all bottled up. She tells me that if she cries every so often it makes her feel better. She has done extensive biblical research that supports the idea that we are not to harbor bitter emotions. One Scripture she loves to quote is, *"A merry heart does good, like medicine, but a broken spirit dries the bones"* (Proverbs 17:22, NKJV). Men, it's all right when your wife just needs to get it out! That is how she is made.

Besides being the more emotional side of the union, women love to talk. On average, they will speak at least twenty-five thousand words a day, sometimes with gusts up to fifty! Men speak an average of twelve thousand words a day, sometimes fewer. Women have a strong need to verbalize. It's their way of communicating. Men communicate, but sometimes it's in grunts.

## He Said...

I think this will illustrate my point. It seems that Rodney was reading the morning newspaper when he came upon a study that said women use more words than men. Excited to prove to his wife, Cathy, his long held contention that women in general, and Cathy in particular, talked too much, he showed her the study results. Rodney read to Cathy, "Men use about 12,000 words per day, but women use around 25,000."

Cathy thought awhile, then said to him, "It's because we have to repeat everything we say."

Rodney said, "What?"

I tell Cheryl, "I'm your best friend, but I'm not your girl-friend. I fail miserably as a girlfriend." If I try to be something I'm not, Cheryl is disappointed in me and I'm disappointed in me. My wife always wants all the details. Not me. Give me the headlines in a newspaper so I know what's going on. I just want the bottom line.

This brings up an important point. Women, be careful who you choose as your close friend. You call up your girlfriend and start unloading on them. "My husband's a dog. He brought me flowers from Wal-Mart on our anniversary. He treats me like a dog. He doesn't do this, he doesn't do that."

Your friend will usually try to console you to make you feel better. That's fine. That's what women do for each other. But be careful when talking to your girlfriends about your hus-band. You may be setting yourself up for failure. Be very care-ful of responses like, "Honey, you know what? You need to leave that man! Just walk out that door and leave him!" This is not the type of friend you need, nor is it the type of conso-lation you need.

## 2 BECOMING 1

Girls appreciate friends who make them feel better. It is natural to want friends who cater to your emotions. This may be what we want, but it is not what we need. This may be a "good" girlfriend, but it is not a "God" girlfriend. Always check motives. A friend may be wrong in her motivation. Check her heart. Because if you leave him and you're divorced, guess who may be having lunch with your ex-husband?

**We all want friends who love us, but we need friends who love us with the truth.** What does the Bible say about your relationship? What does God say that we are to do? It is always easy to see what our mate should be doing, but can you rehearse to yourself what you need to be doing? We all need friends who are willing to risk their friendship with us to tell us what God says we need to do, instead of always focusing on what someone else – in this case, our mate – needs to do.

Men, you have to understand this. Your wives are going to talk. They're created to talk. It's like they've got WD-40 on their jaws. They can talk. They talk about everything and anything. They'll talk to everyone and they can talk about it fast. This is not a flaw in their makeup. It's the way God has made them! We need to learn to celebrate this in our mates.

One night, Cheryl and I went into a hotel room. Before I knew it, the man who brought our bags up at two o'clock in the morning was sitting on the edge of our bed telling my wife his whole life story!

When we go through an airport and my wife sees a ladies' room, it's like an irresistible force. She's drawn like moth to flame, and off she zooms to the "sanctuary." She may spend twenty minutes in there! I don't spend twenty minutes in the restroom. I'm in. I'm out. I'll be standing there, waiting for my

46

wife, when all these women will come out, smiling in my direction.

"Oh, your wife is the sweetest woman. While we were in there she was telling me how to get my son saved."

"While we were in the restroom, your wife gave me a corn-bread dressing recipe."

Meanwhile, I'm holding my wife's purse, muttering to myself in the middle of the airport. When she emerges, I say to her, "That woman over there with the blue shoes told me you gave her a recipe in there."

"What woman?"

"The woman over there with the blue shoes."

"Oh, yes! So that's what she looks like. I never saw her face, just her feet. The cutest blue shoes. There she is. Aww! Praise God. That's wonderful!"

I don't get it.

She doesn't even need to look at the person she's talking to. There isn't a man alive who would carry on a personal conversation in the men's room. We walk in, looking forward (there's no looking around in the men's room), we do our business and we walk out. Men don't talk in the bathroom. If another man wants to carry on a conversation, it will not take place in the men's room!

Women don't understand why we get so excited at football games. Cheryl says the only time a man can really talk is when he's in a room by himself watching football. He can talk to that TV. He can yell at those referees. He can have a lively conversation with a person who's not talking back.

# 2 BECOMING 1

One night Cheryl said to me, "I just want to spend time with you."

"Okay, Honey, the football game is on tonight. Why don't you come and sit with me and we'll watch the game?"

Well, that wasn't what she had in mind. She doesn't even enjoy football. But because she wanted to spend time with me she agreed to watch the game. So we sat down on the couch. As the game kicked off, she began to talk to me.

"What do you think about...?"

"No, no, no, no. There's no talking during the football game. Just watch the game, Honey."

Blissful silence. Only commentary and whistles blowing.

Eventually, a 60-second commercial came on and I said to Cheryl, "Okay, now you can talk." Right away, I knew her conversation was going to take more than 60 seconds. I knew it would take more than four minutes. It was a halftime story! So I cut her off. "Honey, let's save it until halftime, we can talk then."

Through the years, I've learned that sometimes my wife wants to be with me just to be with me. She wants to be with me in any situation. When she's with me, I reach over and take her hand because I know that she wants us to be close. Men, it's okay to watch the football game with your arm around your wife. We enjoy each other's company. Why do so many couples have companionship and intimacy problems when this is such a simple concept?

Try taking your wife's hand or touching her back when you're walking. It satisfies her desire to be touched and it creates a bond between you. Women love to be touched, with no strings attached. When husbands don't touch their wives when sex is not involved, then she may look for a man who will. Many affairs start, not because a woman wants to have an affair, but because she needs someone to talk to her and touch her, intimately, without sex. This is vital for a woman.

*Women need to hear that they are loved all the time.*

Cheryl says that a woman talks to her mate because she needs feedback. She really needs feedback. She wants to know that she is loved and she needs to hear it. "Show" is not enough for a woman; "tell" is much more important.

**Both "show" and "tell" are very important in a marriage.**

Women need to hear that they are loved all the time. Your wife needs to feel it all the time. She needs to know that even if things are going wrong you still won't reject her. If she broke your favorite golf club, threw out your ratty old college sweatshirt and got a $100 speeding ticket, she needs to know your love is still there.

Women need to hear us say the words, "I love you." We think it's good enough that we say it back to them when they tell us, "I love you." In our minds we think, "Why is this necessary? I told her yesterday and I haven't changed my mind since then. Doesn't she remember? What's wrong with her memory?" Or maybe when she says, "I love you," you say, "Ditto." Not a good idea. As providers, we may be under a mistaken impression: "Hey, I bought her this house. She knows I love her!" Not so. To a woman, nothing replaces hearing the actual words. Material possessions do not tell your wife how much you love her.

# 2 BECOMING 1

There is a difference between "I love you," and "I'm in love with you." The first can be said between any two people as a sign of deep friendship. But, "I'm in love with you," is a sign of intimacy which goes beyond that. That little word "in" is the first syllable of in-ti-ma-cy.

Men will give love for sex. Women will give sex for love. These attitudes are both wrong because they are manipulative. The motivation is incorrect. God designed sex for intimacy and oneness. We should give ourselves in intimacy and oneness to our wives because they need it, not because we need to receive something in return. Giving to get is a wrong motivation. Giving for the sake of giving is God's way for us.

Jesus taught that it is better to give than to receive (Acts 20:35). We teach our children this simple idea, but we fail to apply it to our own lives when we actively manipulate one another in our marriage relationship.

Cheryl and I know a woman who has not slept with her husband in a year. She is punishing him. She thinks she is going to change the relationship by trying to control him. Cheryl told her, "He'll change, all right! He'll change his address because you're manipulating him."

My wife has said, "Without physical intimacy in a relationship, you have nothing to build on tomorrow. It's like going to church all your life and never giving Jesus your heart. You're just religious about it. **When you're going through the motions of your marital relationship without God's kind of intimacy, it weakens the foundation.** True intimacy is both physical and spiritual. It involves the soul. If you cannot enter into intimacy with your mate, your marriage is no better than a religious act. You are pretending to be something you're not."

# He Said...

Intimacy is not about sex. It is about communication. *In-to-me-see* is the true definition of intimacy. Opening your soul to your mate, opening your most hidden feelings, opening your heart to let someone else look inside of you, this is true intimacy. *In-to-me-see*. This is an invitation to your mate. "Look inside of me and see who I really am. I trust you to see me as I really am. I trust you to love me just as I really am without pretense, without masks. I trust you not to judge me. I trust you to love me in the good times and in the bad. I trust you with my innermost being."

Men don't generally think like this. Men are motivated by sex. The wonderful thing is that when we finally get beyond our own needs and desires long enough to see the needs and desires of our mates, the physical intimacy follows. But we must keep our hearts clean. We cannot manipulate by giving the emotional intimacy to receive the physical intimacy. Give to give, not to get.

In all the years we've been married, the most important thing I've learned that a man can do for his relationship with his wife is to be willing to change himself and love his wife much more than himself. (See Ephesians 5:24-29 and Colossians 3:18-20.) Intimacy and love are God's gifts to His children. The greatest thing I can do to honor my heavenly Father God is to love and take care of His daughter, His child, my wife!

51

## Chapter Four

# SHE SAID...

❦

## *Cheryl*

God made men and women special and unique. Women, our husbands are not better or higher than we are. Nor are we better or higher than they. We're just very different in the way we approach life. God made male and female in His Image. That's why when we marry and learn to operate as one instead of two, together we have access to all of the personality traits of God.

God is just like both of us. Or more appropriately, since we are His Image and we are His children, we are supposed to be just like God. God Himself encompasses all of the male and female characteristics. **The bond of marriage unifies the male and female characteristics in one flesh, making us more like God than we could ever be separately!** Marriage intertwines the traits of male and female to become one.

Women, don't despise the ways of your husband. He is the way God made him to be, which is basically the opposite of the way you think and feel. But understand that he completes you and you complete him. Together, you are closer to showing forth the image of God.

As we describe the differences between males and females, you might be thinking, "We are the opposite of Harry and Cheryl." Regardless of which mate has which trait, most of the time you will notice the differences. This is what makes each couple uniquely fit together. When two pieces of a puzzle are just alike, they will rarely interlock and rightly fit together. It is the differences that help us fit.

The Bible tells us that when we marry, the two are to become one flesh:

> *And He answered and said to them, "Have you not read that He who made them at the beginning 'made them male and female', and said, 'For this reason a man shall leave his father and mother and be joined to his wife, and the two shall become one flesh'? So then, they are no longer two but one flesh. Therefore what God has joined together, let not man separate."*
>
> Matthew 19:4-6, NKJV

If we fail to become one flesh as the Bible instructs us to do, then we are not utilizing the gift that God gave us. Marriage gives us the absolute opportunity to become more like God. You may be thinking, "Uh-oh, my husband and I must be hopeless because we live together separately. He does his thing, I do my thing. We love each other, but we don't think, act, feel and move as one. What's wrong with us?"

## She Said...

Think for a moment about your marriage relationship. You and your mate are probably walking more in oneness than you realize. I have a revelation that can set you free. Look at that Scripture again: *"...the two shall become one flesh."* Remember that the word *become* is progressive. We are ever becoming one with our mate! It certainly does not happen overnight. It can't. It isn't possible. We continue to perfect the act of becoming one throughout our marriage. Just as in many other areas of life, if we think we've arrived, and there's nothing else we need to change or work on, then that's typically when we need the most work. If you and your husband are actively praying together and working on celebrating your differences instead of just tolerating them, you have found one of the keys to success. Remember, becoming one with your spouse is progressive.

If you are not married, take these words to heart as you seek God for His wisdom in selecting a mate. We believe that it is significant to note here that who you decide to marry is an extremely important decision that should be considered with much prayer and much time spent with that person. Harry and I tell young people all the time, "When you marry and truly become one with your mate, you will become everything that he or she is. This encompasses their family, their upbringing, their beliefs – everything." Now, that's food for thought! Choose wisely!

Many people ask, "How do you become one flesh?" I always answer, "It can be difficult. The first thing that has to happen is that we must learn to trust our mate more than ourselves."

Learning to trust can be very difficult. Many women have been abused by men in their lives. When I ask women in my ministry workshops to stand if they have been abused, 70-80% of the women stand for prayer. Those of us who have been through any kind of abusive situation, whether sexual, physical, mental, verbal, emotional or divorce, know that it leaves deep, painful scars and broken trust. If you are in an abusive relationship, seek godly counsel and, if need be, remove yourself from the imminent danger. Just as there is never justification for abusing someone, there is never justification for suffering abuse, either.

Abuses from our past can make us distant and non-trusting. However, if we cannot allow ourselves to trust our mates, then we can never become one flesh with them. For clarification, I am not talking about trusting someone who is abusing you. I am talking about trusting your mate in your godly marriage relationship, where abuse has no place.

So first we have to choose a mate wisely, then we must learn to trust that person with our lives. If we as humans had all the characteristics of God, male and female, we would not be able to handle it. That's why God split up His personality traits between the male and the female. It would just be too overwhelming for us as humans to have God's total personality housed within us. God can handle it, but we cannot.

This is the ultimate test of choice. This earth's experience is all about humanity's freedom to choose. **It is in the realm of our own choice to operate as one with our spouses.** For this to happen, both parties must choose this course of action. The power of our relationships lies in the choice to become one.

Satan knows that when men and women do not become one flesh, he has an open door of division in their lives. If he can break up the family, he can destroy the foundations of churches and nations. Because the family is the foundation of our society, it is a target for Satan. If he can destroy that foundation, he has a tremendous stronghold on our nation. Sadly, he has done a good job of creating division and divorce. Even if a couple chooses to stay married legally, but they are divided in their hearts, the enemy has still won the battle.

We must get back on our knees before the Father, asking Him to help us restore our marriages. Satan has infiltrated our families, causing perversion, divorce and abortion. We have to stop talking about these issues and get serious about solving them in the spiritual realm. We need to be doers of the Word, not just hearers (James 1:22). I am not saying that I can choose for anyone else. Just keeping my own life submitted to the will of God and my own thoughts and actions in line with God's will is a fulltime job!

*The time has come to put our words into action and fight for the union of marriage, starting with your own!*

Each of us must take responsibility for our own lives, knowing that when we stand before God, the only thing that we will be judged for is our own choices.

The time has come to put our words into action and fight for the union of marriage, starting with your own! You may say, "Cheryl, my marriage is perfect. We have no problems." I say, "Good. Praise God. Now, put on your armor and war in the Spirit on behalf of your neighbor, because according to statistics, 50% of marriages in this country end in divorce!" We need to pray and take back our families and our society. We need to ask God to teach us how to be the women and the wives that He has called us to be. Reading Proverbs 31 in its entirety is a great place to start.

Maybe you have been divorced. Maybe you tried everything and gave everything and your marriage still didn't make it. Well, I have some good news! It's time to be healed! It's time to start living again. God brings everything into the light so it can be healed. He doesn't hide things that need healing. Now, I am not saying that you should go back and try to fix a dead marriage once it has been finalized in divorce. No! God's Word says plainly in Philippians 3:13-14 to forget those things which are behind and look forward to those things which are ahead. His Word says to not remember the things behind us, but to forget about them!

We are not to despise what we have gone through, but we are also not to try to go back there. We are to press forward, not looking back, and not thinking back. Isaiah exhorts us to look up and behold the new thing that He is doing in our future!

*Remember ye not the former things, neither consider the things of old. Behold, I will do a new thing; now it shall spring forth; shall ye not know it? I will even make a way in the wilderness, and rivers in the desert.*
Isaiah 43:18-19, KJV

Maybe you feel like saying, "Cheryl, my future can't be bright! Look at what I've been through!"

I say, "The Lord has plans for you!" Read Jeremiah 29:11. *"For I know the thoughts that I think toward you, says the LORD, thoughts of peace and not of evil, to give you a future and a hope"* (NKJV). Dwell on that Scripture for a while and begin to see your future as God sees it! Relax, smile, laugh a little.

## She Said...

I enjoy making people laugh because when they laugh, they let their walls down. I can aim at myself, my accent or hilarious events that have taken place in my own life, just to help people drop their guard. Even if it's for five minutes, it feels good to let our walls down. But joking around at someone else's expense is not funny. While it's true, life is funny sometimes, we should never make jokes at the expense of our mates. This is hurtful humor. When we laugh at our husbands, it can belittle them, causing strife and division in the relationship.

Men, laughing at your wife's expense can wound her deeply. I dislike sarcasm because I believe that sometimes there is an element of perceived truth behind those sarcastic remarks. Too often, the person using sarcasm at another's expense is taking the opportunity to cruelly insult someone under the thin disguise of a "joke."

Speaking from experience, women hate to be the brunt of a joke, especially in front of a group of people. When men stereotype women and joke about us, it hurts. When we think of all the times we've laughed at men we have to understand that it hurts them, too. We should always say good things about our husbands.

Those of you who have seen Harry and me and have listened to us speak know that we sometimes poke fun at each other. We tell funny stories about each other and sometimes it does seem to be at the expense of the other. But don't be confused. We are operating as one now. We have worked through the initial stages of our relationship, when pride and ego seemed so important. As we are led to tell certain stories that may seem to be at the expense of the other, you need to understand that we have discussed ahead of time what we are going to tell. And we only do so when we believe it will help others to grasp a point we are trying to make.

## 2 BECOMING 1

Even after all these years of working together, we still discuss what has been said to make sure we never cross the line when it comes to one another's feelings. Respect for one another is the key that helps tremendously in this area of understanding.

We all should keep these Scriptures in our hearts and in our mouths to save ourselves from the agony of speaking and hearing hurtful words.

*The more talk, the less truth; the wise measure their words.*

Proverbs 10:19, MSG

*There is that speaketh like the piercings of a sword: but the tongue of the wise is health.*

Proverbs 12:18 , KJV

*He who guards his mouth preserves his life, but he who opens wide his lips shall have destruction.*

Proverbs 13:3, NKJV

*A gentle answer turns away wrath, but a harsh word stirs up anger.*

Proverbs 15:1, NIV

*Congenial conversation – what a pleasure! The right word at the right time – beautiful!*

Proverbs 15:23, MSG

*Pleasant words are as a honeycomb, sweet to the mind and healing to the body.*

Proverbs 16:24, AMP

*He who has knowledge spares his words, and a man of understanding has a cool spirit. Even a fool when he holds his peace is considered wise; when he closes his lips he is esteemed a man of understanding.*

Proverbs 17:27-28, AMP

*He who answers a matter before he hears the facts – it is folly and shame to him.*

Proverbs 18:13, AMP

*A gossip betrays a confidence; so avoid a man who talks too much.*

Proverbs 20:19, NIV

*Better to live on a corner of the roof than share a house with a quarrelsome wife.*

Proverbs 21:9, NIV

*Better to live in a desert than with a quarrelsome and ill-tempered wife.*

Proverbs 21:19, NIV

*A quarrelsome wife is like a constant dripping on a rainy day ...*

Proverbs 27:15, NIV

*Do you see a man who speaks in haste? There is more hope for a fool than for him.*

Proverbs 29:20, NIV

*Do not let any unwholesome talk come out of your mouths, but only what is helpful for building others up according to their needs, that it may benefit those who listen.*

Ephesians 4:29, NIV

Take the time to look up these Scriptures, mark them in your Bible and let them sink into your heart. It is well worth it!

# 2 BECOMING 1

I was recently invited to a bridal shower where the bride-to-be asked for marital advice from all the godly women in attendance. She sat right down in the middle of the floor and said, "I want you to tell me everything you can think of that will help me be a good wife." One of the oldest women there said, "Don't ever, ever, ever let a negative word come out of your mouth about your husband."

I thought to myself, "Lord, that's going to be difficult, because this girl is going to know more negative things about her husband than anyone in the world. She is going to see it every day. She's going to live with it, sleep with it, and eat with it every day." That must be one of the most powerful words of advice that anyone has ever given a bride. Guard your tongue and don't let a negative word ever again come out of your mouth about your husband! If you can't think of anything good to say, then keep quiet until something positive comes to mind! We need to stop rehearsing the bad and start rehearsing the good.

We must learn to accept our husbands and the other men in our lives – fathers, brothers and sons – the way God made them. If we can quit trying to change them to fit our mold, we'll be much happier. When we work on changing ourselves instead of harping on them to change, we will find that we get along with them better and enjoy their company more. Soon the friction and conflict that is churning within us will come to a grinding halt. This is how you win the battle in your own mind!

When we start to operate under these principles, our mates will usually follow suit. But **regardless of anyone else's change or lack of it, our own sincere desire to allow the Lord to change us is the true key.** Our decision to change must be based on our own relationship with the Father, not on other motives. "Lord, change me."

# She Said...

Women are sometimes illogical; at least, our logic is often different from men's. Both attributes have their pros and cons. Naturally, as a woman, I don't consider being illogical a detriment at all. It's a wonderful characteristic. In fact, sometimes I wonder if maybe God loves us more because He made us illogical. Do you know why? Well, when God gives us a word, how often is it logical? Washing seven times in a river probably didn't seem like a logical idea to the leper. (See Second Kings 5:9-11.) He must have thought, "Why not go and wash once? Why not just lay hands on me? Why this river and not that river?" But God's instructions were illogical to the finite mind. "Go, wash yourself seven times in the Jordan, and your flesh will be restored and you will be cleansed." It made no sense, but the end result was an incredible miracle! If everything were logical, it wouldn't take submitting our minds, wills and emotions to obey!

The things of God can seem very illogical. Take faith, for instance. When you exercise your faith, you go against what you see, hear, taste, smell and touch. Exercising faith means going against what you can perceive with your senses. In fact, the Word says, *"...faith is the substance of things hoped for, the evidence of things not seen"* (Hebrews 11:1, KJV). That's illogical, isn't it? When our husbands tell us we're illogical we can just say, "Why, thank you so much! Praise God! I'm so glad, because illogical thinking can be faith in action!"

One of the greatest aspects of being a woman is that we have the ability to turn our logical thinking off and on at will! We can be just as logical as our husbands, and that's the beauty of it. We can change from being illogical to logical! Men, on the other hand, are stuck. It's difficult for them to be illogical; as a result, it's sometimes difficult for them to put faith and trust into action. I am not saying that they can't do it. I am just noting that it takes effort on a male's part to do certain things that come naturally for a female.

Women, it's up to us to be understanding, not angry or upset, if the men in our lives appear inflexible or rigid in matters of faith and trust. It's not their relationship with God that's in question. Not at all! It's simply that men often need to reason out the who, what, when, where and why of a situation before they can trust it or put stock in it. For women, it's as simple as saying, "All right. If you say so, that's good enough for me." We trust, sometimes to a fault, in the natural realm. It's how we're made. Our husbands scope everything out before trusting. That's how they're made. There is a balance to be discovered. Remember, it's called the act of becoming one.

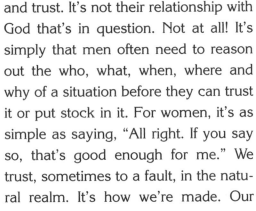

*Women love details, but men want the overall picture.*

Women love details, but men want the overall picture. Give them the bottom line. For instance, when I return home from a conference and my husband asks how it was, what he's really asking is, "Did you buy anything and how much did it cost?" That's what he really wants to know.

On the other hand, when I get home from a conference, I immediately start talking about the meeting as soon as I walk through the door, beginning with the minute I got in the car that morning!

"Well, I got in the car and I closed the door on my dress. I dragged it for 60 miles! Oh, I saw Ann out in her yard."

My brave husband may try to keep up with me here and ask, "What did she say?"

## She Said...

"I don't know. I just waved at her and went on by."

I can see Harry thinking to himself, "What did that have to do with anything?" But, still, I press on. I'll go on from there to tell him where I stopped and where I didn't stop, who I saw and didn't see. What they were wearing. How many Starbucks treats I had. How at one red light there were three cars on the right and two on the left.

At this, he jumps in and asks, "What happened?"

"Hmm? Oh, nothing, I just drove through."

By this time, he has given up completely, tuned me out and gone back to the peaceful refuge of the TV.

The greatest lesson I learned through these types of conversations was not to ask my husband to be my best girlfriend. I'm not saying that he can't be my most wonderful and closest friend, but God did not create my husband to be my detailed listener. Every woman needs one good, true girlfriend because she's the one on the edge of her seat, waiting anxiously to hear all those details. Our husbands don't want to hear the minute details, but our girlfriend can't wait to hear them! Divulge the details to your girlfriend. This will keep your husband from being angry with you, tuning you out and thinking that you're just scatterbrained. This one action can greatly simplify your life.

So, when he asks how the conference went, just tell him what you bought and how much you paid for it. He'll be so excited that he might actually ask you another question about it. It's not that your husband doesn't care about you or the details. He does! He just wants them one question at a time. So do yourself and him a favor by keeping answers short and to the point. Give him the headlines and not the small print. If he wants more, he will ask for it. Understand that this is how he was created. You wouldn't want him to be exactly like you, and vice versa.

Updating a light fixture or replacing an old kitchen faucet with a modern one can change the look and feel of the whole room. It's all in the details! **In marriage, it's also the small details, the little changes here and there that can customize your relationship.** It's all about communicating and realizing that it's our differences that make our relationship great! You'll find that making your relationship smoother and free of conflicts and misunderstandings can create more quality time for you and your spouse to spend together. Time spent arguing or even in angry silence is such a waste! This is your mate. Communicate and celebrate each other's differences.

Communicating this way can be very time consuming, but it is worth it. The benefits outweigh the sacrifice. Our husbands can't listen at the speed we talk, nor can they follow us when we go in all directions at once!

Harry and I often say that women are like computers and men are like filing cabinets. For example, I can get started on something in the evening and run that program over and over, working on every detail, especially when Harry and I are lying down to go to sleep. I can hash it over and over in my mind; but once I vocalize what I'm thinking, Harry is wide-awake and angry at me because now his mind is reeling just when he was about ready to fall asleep. I can go over it for a few minutes and then I'm ready to go to sleep, having solved the crisis in my mind. But my husband is now furious with me because he is wide-awake and wired up! He looks at me, all peaceful and settled into my pillow and just sighs, knowing that he will be awake for hours while I have deleted the problematic file from my "computer" and am now ready for a good night's sleep! I don't set out to ruin my husband's night. But I want his input, so I casually mention what's on my mind. I just need to work on the timing. It's all part of our communication and learning about our differences.

Harry, who is a typical male, puts things in his "filing cabinet" until he is ready to deal with them. When he's ready, he pulls the problem out of the file, studies it and figures out what he is going to do. He doesn't do this in advance, because he rationalizes that the problem may never actually come up. Men tend to think that there is no reason to solve a potential problem. They just wait to see if it ever arises. Then, if it does, they deal with it.

Women figure things out about 15 months in advance. When we come to the situation, we've rehearsed it a million times and know what we're going to do. Just remember, if you have to rehearse it over and over, go off by yourself to do it. God is waiting to hear all about it. Tell Him about it. Work it out and then go to bed. But don't do that to your husband and don't get mad at him when he files things away. Accept that this is the way God made him.

The concept of submission has negative connotations. The world has made it into a negative word. Actually, submission is one of the most positive words in the Bible for women. Right now, you're probably thinking, "You have no idea!" Oh, but I do! I'm married to a strong, confident Lebanese man. Believe me, I know! Don't get me wrong, one of the most attractive traits my husband has is his strength and confidence, but it can come across in an offensive manner, if I let myself perceive it that way. I never said it was easy, but submission is vital to being the woman God called us to be, whether we like it or not. God has already planted flexibility and adaptability inside every female. Remember that He equips those whom He calls:

*Now may the God of peace [Who is the Author and the Giver of peace], Who brought again from among the dead our Lord Jesus, that great Shepherd of the sheep, by the blood [that sealed, ratified] the everlasting agreement (covenant, testament), strengthen (complete, perfect) and make you what you ought to be and equip you with everything good that you may carry out His will; [while He Himself] works in you and accomplishes that which is pleasing in His sight, through Jesus Christ (the Messiah); to Whom be the glory forever and ever (to the ages of the ages). Amen (so be it).*

Hebrews 13:20-21, AMP

Do you know that women are more likely than men to come forward in meetings to receive their healings, their salvation, their touch from the Lord? As women, we have an automatic receiver placed within us. Think about the conception of a baby. Women receive the seed from a man in the act of conception, not the other way around! With that same sort of built-in capacity, it comes more naturally for women to submit to God's will and to receive His instruction for our lives. Please don't misunderstand what I'm saying here. I'm not saying that a man can't be submissive to the Father or receive healing. Absolutely he can! I am simply saying that God has equipped women with what it takes to be submissive. That doesn't make it easy, but it does make it scriptural.

I want to be clear on this subject. The Bible does not instruct women to be submissive to all men. The Bible instructs wives to be submissive to their own husbands (see Ephesians 5). That's something we must remember. The Bible does not teach me that I have to be submissive to all men on earth. But it does tell me that if I'm going to marry, then I need to be submissive to my own husband. Submission is a choice, just like everything else on this earth. God does not force me to submit, but He does give me the choice to obey or disobey. This is His will for my life and my marriage. It is His desire for my life. So for me to choose not to submit to my husband is to choose to disobey God's will for my life. That is just not an option for me! I choose to be submissive to my husband, in accordance with the Word of God.

*Submission is a choice, just like everything else on this earth.*

Now, I am not saying that learning submission was easy for me. I had a career and a life of my own before I became a wife! I ran a company and I took care of my business dealings, my household, my checkbook. And I did not cease to be a wise, valuable person, capable of making intelligent decisions, when I married. I think that's where the idea of submission gets derailed. People often fail to realize that submission is God's idea, not man's. It certainly is not easy, but just as becoming one with your mate is a work in continual progress, submission is a progressive action, too. I honestly wonder if I could have done it with the right heart had I not received a personal revelation of God's plan in this very area of my life and marriage.

The Lord showed me in the Word exactly how He intended marriage to be. Paul wrote: *"Wives be subject (be submissive and adapt yourselves) to your own husbands as [a service] to the Lord"* (Ephesians 5:22, AMP). Look carefully at these words. Wives are to be subject, be submissive and adapt ourselves.

Do you know what the word *adapt* means? One dictionary definition is "to be flexible." Wives, be flexible. The good news is that women are naturally flexible. That's why we have the babies! It's the way God made us. Men are more rigid and inflexible. That's their God-ordained design.

Think about it like this. A spaghetti noodle is hard and brittle before it is boiled in water. It's unbendable. If you try to bend it, it will just break into pieces. But when the water is applied to it with much heat and with a little time, it becomes flexible, bendable and pliable. God has applied the fire of His presence and the water of the Spirit. When you get the fire and the water together and give it a little time, the spaghetti noodle becomes much more flexible. This is what happened to the female, making her the more bendable, adaptable, flexible one.

Men are like the spaghetti noodle without the heat – unbendable. Women are flexible, like the noodle after it has had the water and the heat applied. That analogy clears up the concept for me. I laugh and say in women's meetings, "Be careful when you try to bend a man; he might just break off!" Poor thing, he just can't do it. A woman goes with the flow of the kids, the husband and the lifestyle. That's just the way God made us. Isn't God's perfect design amazing?

You may be thinking, "This is just too hard. That's not the way I am naturally!" You're right. It's not natural, but it is supernatural. God has given us a choice. The ability is in His strength, not in our own. When we make the decision to become the women He has called us to be, and not to be the women that situations, circumstances and our pasts have made us to be, we can relax and enjoy life.

## She Said...

I view life as a spiral; the right choices we make keep us spiraling upward toward our eternal destiny. When we choose to go against the pattern God has designed for us, we are choosing a much more difficult path! But we can choose again. We can begin anew by making new choices. Remember, it's a woman's prerogative to change her mind! Being submissive is hard, but it is part of our supernatural structure. We are handcrafted by God in our makeup and design in a way that makes the seemingly impossible possible.

A submitted attitude must be attained spiritually. I am not sure that submission can be achieved without our minds, wills and emotions being "put under," allowing our spirit man to rise to the top!

Now, don't forget that God said, *"Wives, be flexible to your own husband."* Remember, you are to be flexible and submissive to your own husband, not to men in general. This is not an issue of gender; it is a design just for marriages. I want to obey God, so I choose to be submissive. I didn't really understand why God had set this pattern until I meditated a little more on the Scriptures.

Many times I prayed, "I can discipline myself and make myself submit, God. But it sure would be easier if You would show me the reason why." That's just my nature. I'll do a thing regardless of what I think because I'm disciplined and because I have chosen to obey. But if I have a reason, it certainly makes it easier. When I reread the Scripture in Ephesians, I finally saw it and understood it.

God said, "All right. I'll give you a reason. Read the rest of the verse." It says, *"Wives be subject... to your own husbands as [a service] to the Lord"* (Ephesians 5:22, AMP). I was stunned when I understood that God was giving wives this great opportunity to serve Him through our choices to submit!

God was asking me to be submissive to my husband as a service to the Lord. A service is a favor. I was to submit to my husband as a favor to the Lord!

A favor to the Lord? Absolutely! I will do it for the Father. Harry may not deserve it every day. He may not act like the type of person who deserves a submissive wife, but it is not about Harry. The Word doesn't teach wives to be submissive to their own husbands as a favor to the husband! We are to do it as a favor to the Lord!

*God did not ask us to be submissive to our husbands because they deserve it.*

God did not ask us to be submissive to our husbands because they deserve it. It has nothing to do with whether the husband deserves it or not. This is the first choice given in relationships, and it is given to the wife to choose!

**God asks us to choose to submit so that He can dwell in the middle of our relationships – so that He can be the divine connection in our homes, our marriages and our families.** God's desire is for us to have godly homes and families. Wives, we hold the key! In this one instance, we really are in the driver's seat. It is up to us to start the process, to plant the seed and invite God into our marriage, all by our act of submission. He is triune, and when we open the door for Him in our marriage relationships, then that union becomes triune, too! Now we can truly be formed as one in His image, not just in our own likeness.

## She Said...

With this revelation, we can submit regardless of how our mates act. We can do it regardless of their attitude. We can do it regardless of their faith level that day, because we're not doing it for them; we're doing it for the Father. That makes it so much easier! There will be days when you simply do not want to be a submissive wife to your husband, and there will be days when he simply doesn't deserve it! On those days, remember to do it for the Lord. Do Him a favor.

There are days when I'm completely exhausted when I finally fall into bed. I work at home, doing much of our ministry dates' phone calling, paperwork and trip planning from our house so I can be with the kids. I homeschool, and that's hard work. Working at home is not fun and games, like some people seem to think it is. It can be hard to wear 40 hats all at the same time. Sometimes I can't even figure out which hat I have on! It's difficult. By the end of the day I find myself saying, "I'm not overwhelmed, I'm just in great demand!"

A mother's work is never done. Homeschool or not, when the school day is done, the homework begins. That can make the mom feel like she's the one back in school again! When our children were younger I fed, changed and bathed the baby, prepared dinner for the family, straightened the house and completed the laundry – all while helping with homework. Sound familiar?

Once the kitchen is cleaned up from dinner and the kids are settled into their evening, it is finally my turn to have the bathroom to myself, to try to relax for a moment, while soaking in a warm bubble bath. How wonderful! Only there's no more hot water. We're also fresh out of privacy.

As soon as the bathroom door closes and I disappear from sight, suddenly everyone wants me and can't possibly get by for 10 minutes without me. If I lock the door, the kids think something is terribly wrong and stand outside the door crying until it's finally unlocked. I hear shrieks of, "Mom, where are you?" followed by my husband's voice drifting up the stairs to my sanctuary. "Honey, what are you doing?"

Amazingly, I manage to get a bath, which only takes about a minute because I'm so tired I don't even care if the water gets past my knees. I resign myself to, "Oh well, that's good enough. It's just not worth it to try to squeeze out a few moments to myself anymore."

I step out of the lukewarm tub, throw on some pajamas and emerge from my room, and the very sight of Mom immediately solves everyone's crises. I read to my precious ones and get them to sleep; this seems to take an unspecified amount of time each night that's impossible to predict.

I finally sink into my own bed, trying to be very still and quiet, thinking to myself, "Maybe he won't even notice that I'm here." Now, this has nothing to do with my love for my husband. I love him dearly. I'm just mentally and physically exhausted. I am tired from having to meet everyone's needs all day long. I just need a moment or two of peace, real peace, with no one demanding my attention, my assistance or even my presence in the room.

Just about the time I've relaxed every muscle in my body and have nearly fallen asleep, I feel this hand on my arm. I wonder what that means? My standard answer is just, "Yes?"

That's not, "Yes," in the form of consent. It's "Yes?" in the form of a question! At this point, you're pretty sure what the question is going to be. My husband's question is not always what you might think.

## She Said...

My darling husband will ask me, "Are you hungry?" Well, sometimes I am, but I'm so tired I can't even think about food.

I always say, "No, I'm not hungry."

"Well, I'm hungry."

Now we get to what the first question really meant. It was not to ask if I was hungry. In fact, it is not really a question at all! It is a statement. "Are you hungry?" really means, "I'm hungry and what do we have that you can get me to eat?"

At this point, I try to be a good, submissive, sweet wife because I know I would do this for Jesus. I ask myself what I would do if He were standing there telling me He was hungry. Of course, we know what we would do for Jesus. And it would not be with a negative attitude or any ill feelings.

"Okay, honey. What would you like to eat?" Then here come the questions that I don't think I'll ever understand.

"What do we have? What's in the kitchen? What sounds good to you? Hmmm. I don't know. What do you want?"

Now, my husband does all the grocery shopping (thank you, Harry Salem), so he should know what's in the house! Do we both live in this house? Do we both not have to go through the kitchen to get upstairs? I didn't want anything in the first place, yet now I have to reel off a menu.

So I start naming things that are in the fridge.

"No. I don't want that. No, that doesn't sound good."

We progress to the cabinets.

"No, I'm not in the mood for that."

And then a face, "No, that doesn't sound good."

By now, I want to say, "You're not hungry. If you were hungry you would have taken any of the things I named!" But I say nothing.

I finally drag myself out of bed and go downstairs without turning on the light. If I don't turn on the light, maybe I won't entirely wake up. So I do all of this in the dark. The whole way down the stairs I'm saying, "Father, if You were hungry I would be getting this for You." And trust me, it helps. Because if Jesus asked me to go fix Him a sandwich in the middle of the night, I would jump out of bed and run down the stairs! I would be so excited. So remind yourself of this the next time your husband asks you to serve him.

Loving is natural for women. Providing is natural for men. If you read the fifth chapter of Ephesians, you'll see that the Bible instructs husbands three times to love their wives, but the Scriptures never have to tell wives to love their husbands. Our battles are more with our mouths and in our attitudes. In verse 25 of that chapter, we read: *"Husbands, love your wives, as Christ loved the church and gave Himself up for her..."* Then, in verse 28 it says, *"Even so husbands should love their wives as...their own bodies. He who loves his wife loves himself."* Then in verse 33, *"Let each man [without exception] love his wife..."*

It is not by accident that God tells the husband the same thing three times. God tells the husband to love his wife. Then, three verses later, the husband has forgotten that he was supposed to love his wife, so God tells him again! The number three is defined as divine completeness, perfection and resurrection. When a husband loves a wife the way God has designed him to do, as Christ loves the Church, there is a power there that can resurrect even a dead marriage and bring divine completeness and perfection.

The battle for the male is to continue to love his wife. The battle for the female is to continue to submit to her husband. It is almost funny how easy it is for a female to love and how hard it is for her to submit. In fact, we will tell our husbands all day long, "I love you, honey. I love you, sweetheart. I love you, darling." Sometimes, they even say it back to us. Isn't that why we say it so much? It is not because we want them to hear it, but because we want them to say it. We need to hear that our husbands love us.

Most of the time, we're telling them just because we want them to say it back. Have you ever told yourself, "I am not going to tell him I love him again until he says it first"? Then we wait a day or so, hoping that it won't be much longer before he says, "I love you." Before long, our thoughts begin to run wild.

"What if he doesn't love me at all? What if he only tells me that he loves me because I tell him? What if he never even thinks to tell me and we never say it again to each other?"

The panic begins to rise! Women must hear those precious words, "I love you." When we feel we can't possibly stand it any longer, we blurt out, "I love you," a little too loudly. Our husbands look at us a little startled, with that expression that says, "What's wrong with you?" They wouldn't dare vocalize it, though. And all is right with the world when they say, "I love you, too." Even though they say it with a chuckle that says, "I have no idea what is going on in your mind, but that's okay. Don't explain it to me."

Women love to love and we love to be loved in return. We love to say it and we love to do it. We love to hear it and we love to express it. Women just love to love. But it's not as natural for the male to express his feelings and thoughts about love. That's why God had to remind him over and over and over, "Love your wife. Love your wife. Love your wife." Three times. Divine completion. Divine perfection. Divine resurrection.

It is natural, however, for a male to desire to provide for his wife. And that is why in our society it is very difficult when we become the providers. I'm not saying that it is wrong for women to go out and work. I myself work outside the home. I work when I conduct conferences. I have a business.

But I have to keep in mind that there is a balance. It is Harry's God-given talent and desire to provide for me. It is his gift; it is natural within him to be the provider for me and for our children. If I take that away from him, I take away his expression of masculinity. When we work outside the home, we have to be especially mindful of the way we speak to our husbands. We must be thankful for what they do for us. Just as we love to love and it is absolute life to us, it is absolute life to them to provide for us. So let's not take that away from them. This is very important. Remember, it is our attitudes and our words that can bring problems for us in our relationships.

Females respond primarily to touch, and males respond primarily to sight. In other words, the male wants his female to look good. Yet after a certain point, the wife doesn't care that much about what the husband looks like. The female might have cared when she first met him. Those things might have been very important once upon a time. She wants him to look nice and she wants him to be healthy, but she's not going to stop loving him if his appearance has changed.

If you've been married long enough, your husband probably doesn't look like he looked when you married him. For instance, most men don't have the same amount of hair on their heads as when they started. Oh, don't get me wrong. They have plenty of hair; it's just not in the same place as it once was! Hair that was once on top of the head is now in the ears, in the nose and all over the body! Sadly, their chests may have fallen into their drawers long ago. And have you ever seen such tiny legs holding up such a big body? But we don't care! It doesn't affect us because God made us, the female, to be turned on by touch. As long as that male will hold our hand, or put his arm around us when we walk side by side, as long as he will hold us in front of the kitchen sink, giving us kisses on our cheeks and nibbles on our neck, we think he is absolutely gorgeous and perfect. We are satisfied by touch, not just turned on by touch.

Husbands, on the other hand, are satisfied by their wives' presence. For instance, Harry enjoys watching sports on television. He wants me to sit on the couch with him. I'm not supposed to say a word. He doesn't want me to ask a question. He doesn't want me to look at him or talk to him. He wants me to sit right there because it makes him feel good, satisfied, for me to just be in the room. He wants me to sit there hour after hour and watch sports that I'm definitely not interested in. And I will do it too, if he will hold my hand! Because I am near him, enjoying his hand in mine, and I am satisfied. That's God's way. We are the way we are by His design.

Since we know that our husbands are responsive to sight, it's very important that we work at looking our best for them. We do it for them. We might think we care for our appearance for our own sakes, but we don't. We do it for our husbands because they are turned on by sight.

# 2 BECOMING 1

Don't be annoyed because your husband is turned on by sight. Be excited about it! When he is turned on, he wants to touch you, and that is what you need. But no matter what you do, always guard your motives. By giving him what he wants, we get what we want. It is said that females give sex to get love and that males give love to get sex. But this is not correct. It ought not to be this way. In our relationships, we should not be motivated by our own needs. When we give anything simply to get something, our heart is not right. It is still about us!

Acts 20:35 tells us that it is more blessed to give than to receive. God sees our hearts when we give; He loves a cheerful giver, one whose heart is in his giving. This kind of giving brings honor to the giver, to the recipient and to our Father God.

> *However, let each man of you [without exception] love his wife as [being in a sense] his very own self; and let the wife see that she respects and reverences her husband [that she notices him, regards him, honors him, prefers him, venerates, and esteems him; and that she defers to him, praises him, and loves and admires him exceedingly].*
>
> Ephesians 5:33, AMP

Remember to respect your husband. When you look good, you are respecting your husband. You're telling him that you notice him. Not one time does the Scripture in Ephesians 5:33 indicate that the husband is to notice the wife. It instructs us, the female, to notice him, the male. We are to notice him – to be aware of him, to regard him, to think of him; to honor him (*honor* in the Hebrew means "to open the door"). We are to prefer him over everyone else, to venerate him and to esteem him, lifting him up with our words, actions, and attitude.

# She Said...

This sounds like the exact opposite of the way we approach relationships today! We think it's the male's responsibility to notice the female, but I believe that kind of thinking is backwards to God's way. We want the men to tell us how great we are, but the Bible says we are to tell the men how great they are. A man needs that affirmation. The woman is to defer to him, love and admire him exceedingly and praise him. That's our job, to help our husbands be the men God called them to be. Their job is to love us and provide for us. Each spouse has a job in the marriage; if we'll just do our part, life will be so much better.

*Women are emotional by nature. Men are physical and rational by nature.*

Women are emotional by nature. Men are physical and rational by nature. Women feel before anything else! Men respond by thinking, or with their physical ability first. It's amazing to me. We usually do everything with our emotions. Men tend to do everything with their minds or physical strength. An unsuspecting husband can make a simple observation in regards to his wife's daily life, and it's as if he had dropped a bomb. After the explosion, he says, "What did I do? You asked me how it looked and I answered. I just said that it's a little tight and maybe you could lose an inch."

He didn't even think about how his words would make his wife feel. He just said it. He never intended to say something that was hurtful. From his perspective, it was just a fact. When our husbands make a statement that cuts us to the quick and we are hurt, we need to close our eyes and think for a second. In his mind, he didn't mean to drop that boulder. He was only answering a question!

Do you know how we should respond? We should just laugh and give them a big hug. We can say that we're sorry that we asked a dumb question that was not fair to them. We need to learn to let things go without internalizing them. Sometimes we can set our husbands up for failure. When we create a situation for them where there's no good answer, we might as well have blatantly picked a fight. We need to remind ourselves that he didn't mean what he said in quite the way it sounded. Even if he did, we are not going to let it hurt our feelings. We need to remind ourselves regularly to quit taking things so personally and emotionally, and embrace the beauty of this God-given relationship. We need to learn to celebrate our mates, rehearsing the wonderful things about them, instead of harboring hurt and bitterness from the past.

When we truly understand how our husbands are made and how they approach life, we will be much happier. It is well worth the effort. I continually remind myself that it is not worth it to be right. I continually remind myself to give in. Making my point does not ultimately bring anything positive into our relationship. It only hurts and destroys the godly marriage that God is trying to give us.

## Chapter Five

# THE BLAME GAME

## *Cheryl*

In too many marriages, both husbands and wives are sure that their way of doing things is the only right way. Then when things don't work out in a given situation, we play the blame game. Each spouse points the finger at the other as the source of all difficulty. The problem is that when we blame our mates, it doesn't really solve anything. Even though the need for change should be obvious, many couples are caught in the tangled web of blaming each other...and destroying their relationships in the process.

Often we are convinced that we are right and that our mate is wrong. We become filled with such a strong sense of self-righteousness that we just cannot bring ourselves to let go of our opinions.

When we blame others for making life intolerable for us, we are not taking responsibility for our own shortcomings, fears and choices. It is always easier to blame someone else than to change our own thoughts and actions. Our first instincts and reactions are to immaturely blame someone else when things don't go well. When we take the low road of blaming others and pointing fingers, any possibility of having a healthy relationship goes out the window. Blame produces death in our minds and hearts, and eventually in our relationships. Refusing to keep our focus on our own faults can cause our marriages to dry up from the root.

> *...because they had no root, they dried up and withered away.*
>
> Matthew 13:6, AMP

**Those who blame their spouse, either verbally or nonverbally, have released a poison that will soon deaden any feelings they have for their mates.** Those receiving the blame will either withdraw or lash out, depending on their personality. Those trying to place the blame will convince themselves that they are right and the other person is wrong. Regardless of who was actually right in the circumstance, the result is the same. Both parties soon grow to dislike the one they have committed to love. Households become battlegrounds. Husbands and wives feel the tension in the air while each one struggles for control.

Blaming each other costs our relationships a lot more than we should be willing to pay. We would never talk to our employers the way we talk to mates because we don't want to lose our jobs. At work, we know there aren't any options; we have to negotiate our positions and work things out. At home, we are careless with the feelings of the people we are supposed to love the most.

The damage we cause our relationships is only part of the problem. When we choose to conduct our lives this way, it stunts our own growth and maturity in the Lord. This is because pride is the root cause of blaming others. We proudly refuse to see our own weaknesses and instead focus on someone else's. In the end, blame produces destruction.

There are many situations in life that are beyond our control. But when we are confronted with things we don't know how to fix, we make excuses or try to defend our position by explaining ourselves. Unfortunately, the first thing we think of doing is to absolve ourselves of any fault. This defense mechanism is one of the ways we try to ease painful situations that we are facing.

I married Harry Salem almost twenty years ago. It was a whirlwind courtship for both of us. Before we met, Harry and I had each decided that we would not marry, but would remain single to better serve God. Then we met, and everything changed.

When we first meet our future mates, we love everything about them, even if we secretly don't like ourselves very much. We are thankful that our mates love us just the way we are, and we silently pray that they will never figure out all of our secrets and our true identity.

We unrealistically expect that somehow all our faults will magically disappear when combined with someone else's in marriage. This is the idealistic expectation that many single people have about marriage. Instead of realizing that there are likely to be conflicts when two people with hurting pasts join together, most couples are sure that their union will produce a bright future. Unfortunately, mixing the baggage of two people with different viewpoints can eventually end up in an explosion, a division or a miserable existence with no hope of a better future. Marriage is about blending two lives together. No matter what the components that make up the two lives, when they marry, these components are thrown into the mix as the two become one.

Several years ago, I was in a TV studio bathroom (yes, God talks to me in the bathroom), and this was written on the wall, "Marriage teaches you loyalty, forbearance, restraint and a lot of other qualities you wouldn't need if you stayed single!"

At the time, I thought it was funny. I wrote it down in the front of my Bible so that I would not forget it. Since then, I have read these words in my Bible many times, hoping to let their truth penetrate my mind. These words are so true – and they are necessary for us to hear if we are to stay on track with the course that God has set before every Christian married couple.

It is important that we shake off the fairytale images of marriage and face the facts of who we are, who our partners are and who we can be when we are blended together. We must see things, not with natural eyes, but with spiritual, hope-filled eyes. When there are changes that need to be made in our lives, we must focus on who we can become, not on who we are now.

*We do not look at the things which are seen, but at the things which are not seen. ...*
                                        Second Corinthians 4:18, NKJV

We are ever evolving into the image of Christ, individually and collectively. There is hope in every situation, every circumstance and every relationship. Don't give up now. It's too soon to give up!

After the newness of our relationship wears off, many differences in our lives begin to surface. We discover that our mates are not who we thought they were. We also discover that we have not been magically transformed into someone completely different just because we got married.

Now we not only have our own previous issues and character defects to deal with, but we also have those of our mates. Now our problems are compounded. This is something we never dreamed would happen. **We thought the magic would effortlessly last forever. But the truth is that when it wears off we begin the journey of discovering the person we married.**

I believe that in our marriage, Harry and I have faced the challenges that most couples face, and then some. My husband and I are completely different. Harry comes from a Middle Eastern cultural background and I come from a Southern background. Harry didn't trust anybody and I trusted everybody! Harry was guarded in his personality and I was everybody's friend.

Through the years, we've laughed as we have pictured the wedding we would have had if our two families had come together. (We didn't have this wedding; we just had a private ceremony with no friends or family.) We imagined that it would have been like *The Godfather* meets *The Beverly Hillbillies*! Combustible culture shock! Of course, I am exaggerating on both sides...a little!

Both of us brought our share of past issues into our marriage. We had no thought of how we would make our marriage work; we just plunged in. When we went through distressing times, we each began trying to change the other. We were both crying out to God, "Lord, please change my mate!"

Amazingly, God did absolutely nothing about the problems we experienced as long as we insisted on praying like this! For some years we trudged ahead, trying to figure out how we could get each other to change – until one day the Lord spoke to my heart.

He said, "Cheryl, today I am going to teach you how to pray for your husband."

I thought, "Finally! Now things will change around here."

God said to me, "Pray after Me."

I said, "Okay, God."

The Lord said, "Lord."

I said, "Lord."

The Lord said, "change."

I said, "change."

The Lord said, "me."

I said, "*What?* Lord, You are not listening to me!" The Lord did not answer me at all. He just started over. "Lord."

So I repeated, "Lord."

He said, "change."

I said, "change."

The Lord said, "me."

I could hardly get myself to say that one little word from my heart. The Lord knew my thoughts and prideful hesitation and spoke to me again. "**Cheryl, you do not have a right to**

**ask Me to change another person. You only have a right to ask Me to change you.** You are missing the fact that since you have become one with your husband, I no longer see you as two individuals. I truly see you as one.

"Second, when you truly ask Me to change you, I will begin to change you. But remember that in My sight, you are one with your husband. While I am changing you, it gives Me legal access to your husband. Because of your union, I can begin to work in his life also. You need to give Me permission to change you. But do not be deceived by this. You are the only one you should focus on. You are the one who needs to submit your entire being to Me and let Me change your life and your future."

*I had to change*

*so we could*

*change.*

Finally, I relinquished my will and prayed, "Lord, change me."

While this was happening, a light came on in my mind. I understood what God was saying to me! I had to change so we could change. I could plant the first seed of transformation by making a choice that could produce the harvest of change in our relationship. A process was started at that very moment that was to eternally alter our marriage and our family. When I received this instruction from the Lord, my focus was completely redirected from blaming Harry to seeking God to change me. Now I ask myself different questions. "What can I do differently to make a change in our relationship?"

One of the biggest obstacles we must overcome as Christians is a lack of understanding. We must realize that Satan continually lies to us to destroy our marriages. He feeds our minds with many, many lies. If we believe the lies that he repeatedly tells us, they will soon become truth to us. If believed, these lies will add bad fruit to our accounts. We must not buy into the lies told by the enemy. We must pull down strongholds and cast down imaginations that try to exalt themselves against the knowledge of God in our lives.

> For though we walk in the flesh, we do not war after the flesh: (For the weapons of our warfare are not carnal, but mighty through God to the pulling down of strong holds;) Casting down imaginations, and every high thing that exalteth itself against the knowledge of God, and bringing into captivity every thought to the obedience of Christ...
>
> Second Corinthians 10:3-5, KJV

One of the things the Lord has revealed to us is that **when we blame our pasts, we excuse our present choices.** The enemy tries to entice us to use our past to predict our future. This is a huge deception! Things from our pasts have no right whatsoever to exist in our present or future. The only way our past lives have access to the present is if we resurrect the dead things that have happened to us. When we are not willing to leave our pasts behind us, it is as though we are pulling dead things around behind us in life. We have to get thoughts of our pasts out of our minds and then have the courage to deal head-on with our present choices.

We had to learn that nothing from our pasts has any place in our present or our future. As this truth was revealed in our lives we had to learn to deal with any unresolved emotional conflicts. If there were any lies, we had to uncover them and deal with them. I am not saying that you have to tell your mate everything from your past. I am saying you must deal with yourself in the light of God's love and forgiveness and learn how to move forward.

We all have negative aspects of our lives that we drag from the past into our current relationships. Past hurts from failed relationships can hinder us if we don't cut that baggage loose. We have to realize that if we are harboring the past through thoughts or daydreams, then they are alive and well as part of our present lives. There is no room for the baggage of the past in your marriage. The only way to be free from the past is to walk in supernatural forgiveness and move on. I say that this is how I counsel: "Admit it and quit it!" I know, it sounds over-simplified, but with God, it can be that simple. Let go of the past. Your future is waiting.

You might be thinking, "But you don't know what happened to me. I can't forgive those people for what they did to me." This is another lie of the devil!

Husbands and wives are afraid to forgive the mates who have hurt them because they are buying a lie from the enemy that, unfortunately, is perfectly rational. The lie is that if we forgive those who have upset us, scarred and wounded us, then they will only repeat the hurtful words and behavior. So we might as well keep ourselves closed off so we can't get hurt again.

This is simply not true. When we embrace unforgiveness in our lives, it does not keep the offender in prison. No! The offender will go on with his life while we are held in our own prison of unforgiveness because we will not turn it over to God. When we refuse to forgive the person who hurt us, we are only hurting ourselves and building huge prison walls in our emotions, minds and lives.

**Walking in unforgiveness is like drinking poison and expecting the other person to die!** The only person who is really hurt when we will not forgive is the person who will not free himself from the past and press forward into the future. When we are truly free from the past, wholeness can be ours.

*Jesus said to him, No one who puts his hand to the plow and looks back [to the things behind] is fit for the kingdom of God.*

Luke 9:62, AMP

When our mates do something that we feel is wrong, we are the judge and jury convicting them and playing the recording of their transgressions over and over in our minds. We think about the words our mate spoke to us, what they did to us and what they will probably do in the future if we can't change them. When we're finished we have thrown ourselves into an inescapable prison. We're the ones who are locked up! And we are the only ones who can unlock the prison doors. This can only be done when we understand that we ourselves hold the key to the prison door — forgiveness.

*Walking in unforgiveness is like drinking poison and expecting the other person to die!*

Forgiveness is not easy. We cannot forgive just by saying the words. Forgiveness is a mental and emotional choice that we make, followed by a spiritual release.

The only way we can truly forgive someone is through the love of God in our lives. It is not possible with mere human ability or strength of will. It takes supernatural ability through the love of God to truly forgive and release someone. The funny thing is that the one who is really set free is the one who is walking in forgiveness. This choice must be made over and over until we finally understand that the episode is over. Forgiveness will give us more freedom than we could ever imagine.

We have to learn to walk in forgiveness in our emotions, minds and wills. Until we can do this, we're not truly walking, living, moving and breathing in true forgiveness. And until we do these things, we cannot progress and move forward. Unforgiveness continually pulls us back to our pasts. Remember the story in the Old Testament about Lot's wife? When she looked back, she was turned to a pillar of salt! She dried up from the inside out. Today, marriages are slowly drying up from their past hurts. The oil and water of our lives is slowly being drained from us and from our relationships until there is nothing left but a dry, useless, pile of salt.

This is not the future God has planned for us. We must make a decision not to blame everyone else around us for everything that happens. We must embrace the promise of the future and run toward that promise. Paul said it best in Philippians 3:13-15 (NKJV):

*Brethren, I do not count myself to have apprehended; but one thing I do, forgetting those things which are behind and reaching forward to those things which are ahead, I press toward the goal for the prize of the upward call of God in Christ Jesus. Therefore let us, as many as are mature, have this mind; and if in anything you think otherwise, God will reveal even this to you.*

We cannot reach forward – we can't even look forward – until we learn to forget those things that are behind. This is the biggest step toward our freedom from blaming others. This step is the first step, the most important step, and it cannot be left out. Without this first step, no other steps can be taken. We have to learn to forget the hurts and wounds of our pasts. We must surrender those hurtful thoughts that we carry around like a badge of honor. It is not honorable to display that badge. In fact, it is the exact opposite of the definition of the word, *honor*. Remember, in the ancient Hebrew, the word *honor* means "to open the door."

We dishonor ourselves by harboring unforgiveness and refusing to set ourselves free from our pasts. We are slamming the door shut on our own futures! We can open the door and go forward without hurt, fear or pain, but it will take much effort. When we refuse this path, the effects are usually devastating.

The apostle Paul said, *"This one thing I do..."* (Philippians 3:13) It takes a lifetime commitment to walk in forgiveness and to forget our pasts. Paul was most probably speaking to some of the very people whose loved ones he himself was responsible for having had put to death. Paul had been a murderer of Christians prior to his salvation. But his statement, *"This one thing I do, forgetting what lies behind..."* reminds us that we must make a conscious effort to forget our pasts and press toward our futures together without blame and unforgiveness crippling us.

Harry and I worked through many hurts, scars and memories together before we arrived at a peaceful resolution. God showed us the pathway to freedom from abuse, depression, rejection and abandonment. He helped us get free of our crippling thought patterns. Today our marriage is whole and we are whole as individuals.

# The Blame Game

It took time to deal with the differences we had, but we came to understand that time was our friend, not our enemy. Time allowed us to change gradually as we were able to deal with our issues one layer at a time. We shouldn't despise the time it takes us to work through our differences. When we are finished, we will realize that it is a tremendously freeing process. **We cannot embrace the promise and ignore the process!**

We are now a whole and free family. We stopped the vicious cycle of blaming each other. Little by little, we learned to operate as one, not just as two people who are legally married. Many people who are married have not achieved true oneness; but when we stop blaming each other, we are on the road to truly becoming one flesh. This is God's design and His best for our marriages, but it will take much effort on the part of both mates.

Please don't misunderstand. Both people in a marriage do not have to change at the same time. One person can decide to break the destructive cycle and start the relationship moving in a different direction. When one person decides to change the pattern and operate in God's love as described in First Corinthians 13, the dynamics of the relationship can change. Because of God's divine plan of two becoming one, it only takes the choice of one to change the direction of both.

Changing is not easy. In fact, it may be the hardest thing you'll ever do. But if we are willing to wait and not give up, if we are willing to not grow weary in well-doing, then we can reap, if we faint not.

*And let us not grow weary while doing good, for in due season we shall reap if we do not lose heart.*
                                                        Galatians 6:9, NKJV

## 2 BECOMING 1

Harry and I have even blended our ministries into a family ministry. We now deliver the message of restoration, hope and healing with two voices. We travel and minister two by two, reaching families one by one. Our sons travel with us, ministering and singing and blessing our lives. We are living a dream come true, but we have overcome tragedy in our lives that we never dreamed would come our way.

Our lives were shattered within moments on January 11, 1999. In shock, we listened to the doctor's diagnosis that our precious five-year-old angel and only daughter had an inoperable brain tumor. We were told that she had only weeks to live and that there was nothing that could be done. It was then that the important work we had done in our marriage really held us together. We battled together and walked together in agreement no matter what decision we had to make. We walked and operated as one regardless of whether the decision was small or life-threatening.

One summer day in July of that year was particularly hard for us to face. In January, we had been told that Gabrielle would not live to see her sixth birthday. But through our persistent faith, agreement and constant prayers as well as the support of God's people, she had a glorious sixth birthday party on May 26th! We tried to keep her life as normal as possible. When her little body could handle it, we would go back on the road preaching. We continually shouted in accordance with Isaiah 42:22, "Restore, restore and restore!" And we believed it.

We were in Michigan when Gabrielle's condition began to deteriorate rapidly. We loaded up the motor coach. As quickly as humanly possible, we headed down the interstate running toward our safe haven, our home in Tulsa.

# The Blame Game

We had only been on the road for a few hours when Gabrielle's condition began to worsen dramatically. We couldn't get her to respond at all. No matter what I gave her, she was turning blue, with only a tiny amount of air going through her body. She was dying as we raced forward, trying not to look back.

I told Harry that we had to do something quickly. He was taking us home. That's all any of us knew to do. We were in the middle of the country, far away from home. We had no local phone numbers and no idea where the nearest hospital was located. We realized that we were close to a church that had been standing with us for Gabrielle's healing and restoration, so I called them. **Miraculously, they were gathered at that very moment in the sanctuary, interceding and standing in the gap for our daughter!** One of the precious church members met us at the exit and escorted us at record speed through the town and toward the nearest hospital.

By the time we reached the hospital, Gabrielle was unconscious. She was immediately intubated and put on life support. A CAT scan revealed our deepest fears. If Gabrielle's condition did not turn around quickly, she had less than an hour or two to live. The medical team had stabilized her, but they did not have a Neonatal Intensive Care Unit at the small hospital, so they put our daughter inside a life-flight helicopter to fly her to an NICU in Kalamazoo, Michigan. I was about to board the helicopter with her when they told me I could not go. There was not room enough for the attendants who were needed to keep our daughter alive. I was devastated at first because I had never left my baby's side, but I recovered and quickly submitted.

## 2 BECOMING 1

My heart was broken. Harry's heart was broken. The boy's hearts were broken. But within moments, we all knew what we had to do. We quickly began pulling together to tear down the strongholds of what we had heard and cast down the imaginations that were trying to take over our minds. We prayed, agreed and strongly stood together as a family.

Harry drove us to Gabrielle as quickly as he could. The life-flight helicopter had arrived much earlier, so when we got there the doctors said that they would need to operate immediately. We were told that the operation would not solve anything or change anything of the original diagnoses, but that it might ease some of the pressure at that moment and give us a few more hours at least.

Harry and I told them we had to pray about it. We went into a small room by ourselves and sought the Lord. Harry spoke first. He rehearsed the facts. This operation would only weaken her further. It would not cure her and it would not help the overall situation. We prayed and sought the counsel of the Holy Spirit. We both felt that the operation was not God's choice for this situation. It would not ultimately change anything. We agreed. We walked out and told the doctor our decision. He reminded us that she would only live for about another hour. We refused to hear this. We tried not to think too much, but to remain in agreement with one another.

An hour passed, then another. Three, four, five hours turned into ten hours! The horrible night was over and she was still with us! The peace of God was all over us, and all over the ICU unit. The attending doctor did not leave when his shift was over. He just stayed there and talked with us. At the time we couldn't know that only a year or so earlier this doctor's three-year-old son had died of the same condition.

98

# The Blame Game

We shared Jesus with him. We loved on him. Our agreement, our strength and peace spoke to him. Gabrielle came out of the coma and they took her off of life support. She continued to breathe on her own. After 36 hours, they told us we could take her home. They had done another MRI. What they had seen on the first MRI that had caused them to give her only an hour or two to live was no longer there! We went home, grateful to God for the priceless gift of these precious minutes we now had.

We fought hard, we battled long, and we stayed in agreement as a family and never broke covenant; but on November 23, 1999, Gabrielle took her last breath on this earth and opened her eyes for all eternity in Heaven. She is not dead, only separated from us. She is alive in Heaven forever. She is not coming back here to us, but we can go to her when our time comes!

Now you might be thinking, "What does this story have to do with blame?"

One of the things that Harry and I have discovered is that when we agree, it rules out any possibility for blame in the future. When we were at the most critical point in Gabrielle's illness, we refused to go back to our old ways of thinking. We stopped, we prayed, we sought the Holy Spirit and we came into agreement. That left no room for either of us to blame the other later. There was no open door to point the finger with accusations of, "You did this," or "You said that..." We made decisions together, leaving no room for blame.

It is not easy to get to this place, but it is vital for healthy relationships. The one who continually blames someone else can eventually find himself sick in the flesh. Unresolved emotional hurts and scars can eventually turn into bitterness, anger or both and make us sick.

We must deal with our own thoughts and bring every thought captive to the obedience of Christ; then we can move toward healthy and whole relationships. (See Second Corinthians 10:5.) We must build toward the future and stop the death trap of looking back!

By letting go of immature ways of thinking, we can get a head start on healthy, godly relationships. The blame game can cost you everything. It is not worth it.

## Chapter Six

# UNITY: WALKING AS ONE FLESH

~

### *Harry*

In the beginning, everything was in God. He contained within Himself all of mankind, the angels and the universe. We know this because the Scripture says, *"...he hath chosen us in him before the foundation of the world"* (Ephesians 1:4a, KJV). There always was and always will be only one God. Unity and oneness were found in the very fabric of His Being.

When Cheryl and I began to study how and why we were created, we gained a better understanding of our relationship with God and with each other. I grew to appreciate why my wife spoke, acted and thought as she did, and it was the same for her. We began to grow in unity.

# 2 BECOMING 1

*Oneness* and *unity* are words that we have been praying about and studying for years. From the time we were first married, we wanted the best God had to give us in our marriage. We have been learning to live our lives in agreement and unity ever since God called us out of two separate ministries and told us to operate and minister as one in one ministry...two voices, one message. **Every day we come closer and closer together in the spirit.** When God gave us this revelation, we were both ready to receive whatever He had for us. We wanted to experience God's unity in our lives and we wanted to share the revelation with others.

The Lord started the revelation by saying, "In the beginning God."

We immediately rushed to finish the thought, "...created the heavens and the earth." But God said, "No!" He wanted us to listen and really understand what perfect oneness really was, not what we thought it was.

"Everything that is, was and will be was in Me in the beginning. *Everything* includes time, space, matter, humanity and even Lucifer. Everything." He continued, "I am One because I am One. I am One by My own design. But I want to have unity and Oneness through relationship with you and by your choice. I want each man and woman to make a choice to come to Me. I don't want you to be 'in Me' by design. I want you to be One with Me – in Me by your own choice.

"In the beginning, I designed all Creation to be in Me. Man couldn't choose Me because he was already in Me. No choice was necessary. There was no power in this, though, no commitment. I want mankind to be in Me because men choose to be there, not because they are there by My own design. I decided to give man a free will, the freedom to choose to love Me or not to love Me. In that choice lies the one true power for all mankind.

"I separated mankind from Me."

This revelation was so different from what we had been taught. As we prayed about it, the revelation began to come to our minds and hearts. When I began to see with my spiritual eyes what God was saying, it shook my mind to the core. The more we thought about it, the clearer and more concise it became. We received the revelation. God wants us to love Him, serve Him and be one with Him because we want to, not because we have to. He does not want us to do it because it's part of His great design. He doesn't want puppets. He wants us to choose to love Him. God doesn't want an arranged marriage for Himself where His lover, His bride, His church has no choice but to give herself to Him. He wants us to choose to die to self and become one with Him.

If Cheryl had had no choice but to become my wife, I could never have been totally sure that she loved me. I would have no real security in our relationship. I would never be sure if she really had become one with me. An arranged marriage is part of a design, not part of a choice. The power of all our relationships, whether horizontal with other people or vertical with God, lies in our ability to choose. Our relationship with God is not by design, but by choice.

I finally realized that this is why male and female must choose to become one and to operate as one.

God takes us as two different people and then, by the choices we make, He fuses us into one flesh in marriage, as we were before God separated us in the Garden of Eden. Man and woman were originally one person; they were separated, and now, by choice, we can become one again. When we both love God, our union must continue for a lifetime.

The true choice of oneness can only be made when we have been born again and when both our lives are committed to Christ. God's kind of oneness does not come from a person declaring we are one. Being legally married here on earth does not automatically make you one in God's sight. Becoming one is a choice that no one can make for you. You alone must choose to die to yourself and become one with your mate. This is the power of agreement.

It is obvious that the man and woman who have truly become one in the Spirit want to continue that perfect unity. The happiness and peace that they have experienced from being one is far superior to what the secular world offers.

We have known some people who were truly one in the spirit. These soul mates cannot imagine how to live on this earth when their mates go on to heaven ahead of them.

Cheryl's paternal grandparents were very spiritual. They lived on a different level than most people. They didn't have much of the revelation that we have today because God had not yet revealed much of what He is showing His church now, in this present day. But they took what God had shared with them in the spirit and they walked in it daily. They were very rarely sick, and never with anything serious.

When Cheryl was about 15 years old, her grandfather began to show signs of skin cancer. Over the next few months, he grew progressively worse. As he grew closer and closer to heaven, her grandmother began to have signs of sickness in her body. This all happened very quickly, within a few short months. They died only two weeks apart, with two totally unrelated illnesses. Neither of them had ever had signs of the illness before. Cheryl believes that they simply chose to be together and they went to heaven just two short weeks apart. They had truly become one here on Earth, as God planned for them to be, and could not stand to live here without each other.

The Lord continued to open our eyes through His revelation. He told Cheryl, "For years you have read and studied Genesis, and yet you've never understood the entire meaning of creation. Creation was intended for the preparation of choice. When I created the earthly realm, I divided. Look at the verses."

Suddenly, in her vision from the Lord, the Bible fell open in front of her. She said the Word came alive, bursting with action and flowing like a mighty river. The river was rushing, cleansing and purifying. Cheryl told me that for the first time in her thirty years of meditation and study of Genesis, she saw the truth.

God told her to look at the verses. We looked at the verses together and were amazed that the truth had been there all the time (Genesis 1:1-27).

First God divided the heaven and the earth.

Then God divided the light from the darkness.

Then God divided the evening from the morning.

Then God divided the waters above from the waters beneath.

Then God divided the land from the seas.

Then God divided the seedtime from the harvest.

In verse 14, we see that He divided the day from the night.

He even further divided the seasons, days and years. This is not the same as dividing the light from the darkness or the evening from the morning; this is the division of the day from the night.

Then God divided the two great lights of the sun and moon.

In verse 18, we see God again dividing the light from the darkness.

Then God divided every living creature that moves, including great sea monsters and every winged bird according to their own kind. He further divided sea creatures below the earth and living creatures on the earth, and winged creatures that fly above the earth. Then God divided the living creatures according to their own kinds: livestock, creeping things and wild beasts of the earth according to their kinds. Then God divided the wild beasts of the earth according to their kinds, domestic animals according to their kinds, and everything that creeps on the earth according to its kind. Then God made mankind in His image. In the image and likeness of God He made them.

First God said it, and then God did it. Or, is it that because He said it, releasing a sound wave, that the action automatically followed the releasing of sound into the atmosphere? Numerous times we have heard from the pulpit that God spoke creation into existence. But have we really thought about what that means?[1]

Scientists have now proven that causing a sound wave to speed up fast enough can cause that sound wave to become light. Think about that! When God *"said ..."* slowing Himself down enough for light to become sound, He produced the elements of creation.[2]

**Scientists have ascertained that the very core of our cells, the smallest part that they can see with a very powerful microscope, is a sound wave.** That makes sense, doesn't it? We are made in God's image, we know that God is light, and we are made from that light. Light, when slowed down, can become sound. The very image of God is mankind, a slowed down image of the Most High God! Mankind is part of God's light wave that became sound. Mankind is a lower and slower image of the Most High God!

*Mankind is part of God's light wave that became sound.*

That does not mean that we are little gods on this earth. By no means! To the contrary, we are only His children when we choose to love Him, when we choose to die to our own desires and live for Him. We have the ability within our makeup, our design, to be in His image. But our choice is what makes the pattern become a reality. I choose God. I choose life. I choose the light of God illuminating my spirit man so that I become His very image, His likeness. I am no more God than my reflection in the mirror is me! It is my reflection, but without the true substance, the finished dimension, of who I am. God uses us who choose Him to be a reflection, a flat image of sorts, of Who He is to the world around us.

In these verses, we read the first part of the division of mankind.

# 2 BECOMING 1

*God said, Let Us [Father, Son, and Holy Spirit] make*
*mankind in Our image, after Our likeness, and let*
*them have complete authority over the fish of the sea,*
*the birds of the air, the [tame] beasts, and over all of the*
*earth, and over everything that creeps upon the earth.*
*So God created man in His own image, in the image*
*and likeness of God He created him; male and female*
*He created them. And God blessed them and said to*
*them, Be fruitful, multiply, and fill the earth, and sub-*
*due it [using all its vast resources in the service of God*
*and man]; and have dominion over the fish of the sea,*
*the birds of the air, and over every living creature that*
*moves upon the earth.*

Genesis 1:26-28, AMP

Notice that God blessed *them*; at that point the male and female were still contained in one body. There was no separation of male or female. They were one, just as the triune God is Three in One: Father, Son and Holy Spirit. God housed man and woman in one body, but God referred to the creation as *them*. They were uniquely individualized, yet they only had one body. The only thing that we can relate this to is like Siamese twins, only more so. Two minds, two spirits, two souls, but only one body.

There were no choices of being one with each other because mankind, the man and the woman, were already one. But mankind was one with each other by God's design, not by their own choice. We know that God named them both Adam (Genesis 5:1). There was no reason to name them two names, because they were one by design.

During creation, God purified Himself and man received the ability to choose to be one with God. Mankind was separated out of God, not as punishment, but as preparation. There had to be a choice. Man must choose to love God, to be one with Him. Creation became all about choice.

After mankind was created, we read in the second chapter of Genesis that the heavens and the earth were finished and rest was ordained. God said, *"It is finished."*

Genesis 2:4,8 explains that the account given is the history of the heavens and the earth and that the Lord God planted a garden called Eden where He placed man (male and female in one body). Then God divided the garden so that the Tree of Life and the Tree of the Knowledge of Good and Evil would be in the center of the Garden. Genesis 2:10 tells of a river going forth out of Eden to water the garden and how it divided and became four rivers.

This revelation has always been there in the Book of Genesis. It is written in black and white. God changed the design of creation so mankind could have countless choices and freedoms. We can choose to receive salvation; we can choose which river we travel, which bird we like and so on. Our freedom of choice is endless!

**God created a world full of many, many choices.** Creation is about choice. I have the freedom to choose whatever I like. God does not choose for me; I choose for myself.

Genesis 2:10 says the rivers out of the Garden of Eden are divided into four *"river heads."* Why would He use the word *heads?* Was it because decisions are made in the head, in the thought process? We think it was because God was dividing everything to prove that the earth and the heavens and mankind must choose to come together as one!

The number four in this verse is important because it describes the world order – north, south, east and west. The four corners of the earth, so to speak, are the divine design of the earth. When we examine Scripture closely, we see that there are numerous meanings that are hidden in the Hebrew language. Studying and reflecting on the Word of God helps us to receive all that He has for us.

Genesis 2:16-17 is the first commandment of God to man. The Amplified Version puts it this way:

> *And the Lord God commanded the man, saying, You may freely eat of every tree of the garden; But of the tree of the knowledge of good and evil and blessing and calamity you shall not eat, for in the day that you eat of it you shall surely die.*

Notice that the first commandment of God instructs us to do what we can do, not what we cannot do. We can freely eat of any of the numerous trees in the Garden, except one tree. We are instructed not to eat of the Tree of the Knowledge of Good and Evil. Only good and blessing are ordained for God's children. *"This is what I have for you,"* says the Father. *"I have ordained good and blessing for you...not calamity and evil"* (see Jeremiah 29:11).

Then God said:

> *Now the Lord God said, It is not good (sufficient, satis-factory) that the man should be alone; I will make him a helper meet (suitable, adapted, complementary) for him.*
> Genesis 2:18, AMP

Remember, until this point, man was a dual being: two persons in one body with triune layers of body, soul and spir-

110

it. Don't be confused here. We are made in God's image, and we are triune beings. Yet, with our natural, physical eyes we see only two parts. How could this be God's image? The link between the spirit and the natural, the merging of the heavens and the earth for all eternity, will only be made with one divine connection, Jesus. The Son of God connects the horizontal to the vertical.

Think about this. The sign of the cross connects the vertical and the horizontal. At the very intersection of the cross is where the head of our Lord and Savior rested. Jesus is the third part of mankind. Only with Jesus between male and female can we truly become the complete image of God on the earth. Is this not the promise of agreement in Matthew 18:19-20?

> *"Again I say to you that if two of you agree on earth concerning anything that they ask, it will be done for them by My Father in heaven. For where two or three are gathered together in My name, I am there in the midst of them"* (NKJV).

So what is the purpose of the separation of mankind? When God said that it is not good that man should be alone, the translated word for *alone* has an enlightening meaning. It means *of each alike*. There is no power when two alike can agree. I have always said that in the context of the marriage relationship, if we are both alike then one of us is unnecessary! It takes both sides, both views, both points, both sights, to make us well rounded and to make us accountable.

Then God separated male and female into two beings. It was at this moment that choice was born. Man and woman must now choose to walk in agreement and to operate as one.

# 2 BECOMING 1

God changed the original design of man and woman so that they must choose to be one, not by design, but by choice! Now if they wanted to walk as one, they would have to make that choice. They would have to die to their own desires and learn to focus on the needs, likes and desires of their mates. By putting oneself aside and learning to live and operate by the needs of the other, we learn how to lay down our lives.

After God divided the male and female into two separate beings, He then took another important step and divided man from God, not just physically, but soulishly, emotionally and, depending on man's choice, even spiritually. In Genesis 2:24, He finished the preparation process for mankind: *"Therefore a man shall leave his father and his mother and shall become united and cleave to his wife, and they shall become one flesh"* (AMP).

Until this time, God and mankind had been united. God now gave man a choice to be One with Him. Now man had to live by his own choices. God created us to be beings of choice, not animals that live by instinct. What will we choose?

Genesis 3:4-5 finds Satan tempting the woman to eat of the Tree of Knowledge of Good and Evil. He lies to her, saying that once she eats of the fruit she will be like God. This would not have been a temptation if Eve had still been united with God. But at this point, she was divided from God and could only return to oneness with Him by her own choice.

It is the age-old problem for mankind. We always want to find the easy way, the shortcut. I remember as a teenager wanting to be told what to do. I hated having to choose for myself. If someone were to tell me what to do, then I could blame the one who chose for me if I didn't like the outcome.

But when I had to choose for myself, I had no one to blame if the decision was the wrong choice.

God had already made a way for His image to be one with Him. It was simple. Man had only to obey God's clear direction. He could eat of every tree in the garden, including the Tree of Life; but he could not eat of the Tree of Knowledge. This would always solidify and finish the relationship. Obedience is always the answer. It is simple...but not usually easy.

The woman's desire to return to Oneness with God may have been so overpowering that she chose a shortcut presented to her by her mortal enemy to return to that God-given relationship. As humans, we desperately dislike waiting. Unfortunately, the earth is all about waiting. Eve gave in and ate the forbidden fruit. Like Eve, we will always have an inner longing to return to our original union with God, but we can never choose the shortcuts of the enemy to reach that goal. God has given us a scriptural way to return to unity with Him.

Adam and Eve must have longed to be one with God again. Yet the Bible says that He came to the garden regularly. The man and woman walked and talked with Him. Satan may actually have made them think they were doing the right thing by choosing to eat of the wrong tree. He may have lied and told them that this was the quickest way back to that great feeling they had experienced when they were One with the Father. No matter what the plot or plan was, both the male and female disobeyed God's command. The Bible tells us that Eve was deceived. Sin entered into the heart of man because of disobedience. The law of sin and death became a legal stronghold in man's existence and Adam handed his dominion, authority and power to the evil enemy, Satan.

## 2 BECOMING 1

We cannot be driven by our feelings. We cannot allow our lives to be led by our five physical senses. **We are to commune with God in spirit and in truth. We can only do this when we choose to crucify our own desires and natures.** Jesus told us that we are not to let our hearts be troubled, that He is the Way, the Truth and the Life (see John 4). From the beginning until today, Jesus is the divine connection for mankind to enter back into union with the Trinity.

With Jesus at the crossroad of our beings, when we can agree as male and female, we can then become the true triune being, the very image of God.

When Eve ate of the forbidden fruit, she forever sealed the fate of Jesus, the sinless, spotless Lamb who would come to take away the sins of the world on the cross of Calvary. She had Him with her already, but her fleshly desire to find an easier way for herself destined the very path, the Via Dolorosa, for Jesus Christ, the anointed One, the Savior of this world.

Some people blame the male, saying that he was with God when He gave the commandment not to eat of the tree and that the female had not been created when that command from God was given. I have heard it said that the female did not even know that she was not to eat. Nothing could be further from the truth. Remember that mankind was both male and female before they were separated. Eve, still named Adam at the time, was right there (Genesis 5:1). She heard the commandment. She knew that this choice she was making was totally and completely against the very words of her God. Yes, the male and female were both present when the instructions were given. They were together in one body, and they both heard the command not to eat of that tree.

# Unity: Walking as One Flesh

What would have happened if Adam and Eve hadn't hidden themselves from God in the garden? What would have happened if they had simply repented at that moment, sincerely asking their Father to forgive them? Had they humbled themselves with broken hearts, bowed on bended knee, met God walking in the garden and begged Him for forgiveness, would there have been a need for Jesus to come to the earth as the spotless Lamb of God? I don't know. But one absolute we do know. God is a God of order and of law. Man legally gave up his dominion, and it would take a legal action from God to reverse the curse of the law of sin and death. We also know that man's first reaction was not to repent, but rather to defend his own sinful choices.

*We must never forget that we were originally created to be One with God and to be one with our mates through our own choices.*

Adam did not take the high road. He began blaming everyone but himself. First he blamed the woman, then he blamed God for giving him the woman. He added insult to injury in an already bad decision because blame always leads to destruction and the curse. Blame and shame always walk hand in hand with pride. But repentance always leads to restoration and the blessing of God. That day Adam made the second worst decision of his life. He did not take responsibility for his own choices; instead, he blamed. He pointed fingers. Pride had taken root in his heart.

We must never forget that we were originally created to be One with God and to be one with our mates through our own choices. God's greatest gift to us is that He wants us to return to Him, with nothing hidden, nothing missing, no shame, no blame...just total acceptance.

Having that oneness flowing through our spirits and bodies is the ultimate spiritual experience. It is reserved for those who eagerly seek God with expectant hearts. Those who are earnestly hungry for more of the Lord can experience the exquisiteness of being One with Him.

*Ask, and it shall be given you; seek, and ye shall find; knock, and it shall be opened unto you...*
Matthew 7:7, KJV

## Relationship Challenge:

*"... do me a favor. Agree with each other, love each other, be deep-spirited friends. ...Forget yourselves long enough to lend a helping hand."* —Philippians 2:2-4, MSG

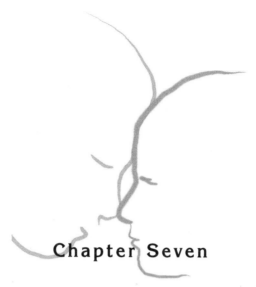

## Chapter Seven

# THE POWER OF AGREEMENT

### *Cheryl*

Harry and I had only known each other for a short time when we married. We would not have considered marrying so quickly, but the Lord impressed on both of our hearts that we were to be together.

We were not like some married couples. From the very beginning of our marriage, we had to work on our relationship. We wanted the fairytale, but instead we got a mystery thriller! We wanted our marriage to be effortless, but this was not the case. From the moment we began our lives together we were challenged.

Within the first months, Harry was promoted to an executive position at work. His weeks were filled with heavy responsibility and he traveled on many weekends. I traveled every weekend from Friday morning through Sunday night and often did not return home until sometime on Monday. I ministered and traveled all over the country weekend after weekend. We had two separate ministries. We had two separate lives.

Like most newlywed couples, we were completely in love. But things began to come between us right away. From our first meeting, one of the things that drew me to Harry was his strength. But I thought the purpose of that strength was to protect me – when I wanted it and when I thought that I needed it. Harry had other ideas. It bothered him that I traveled without him. Yet he was not about to follow me around the country. I couldn't understand it. I thought that he should just trust the Lord.

I have always been very independent. When I was in college, I would tell my parents that I was going somewhere, but I was never closely monitored. Life with Harry was quite different. He wanted me to call him when I left and again when I arrived. I was to be available to him so he could call and talk to me no matter what I was doing. He expected me to be in my hotel room by 10:00 each night while I was on the road. On one hand, I loved that he cared about me and that he was concerned for my safety. On the other, my free spirit rebelled at such close supervision. Now, such control can be a warning sign of a manipulative, controlling spirit and later abuse; but in our case much may be attributed to my husband's upbringing. He was doing what he thought was the right thing at the time. His role, as he knew it, was to care for and protect me, even when he was not physically with me. Yet even though he acted this way out of love and concern, it felt like control to me!

Harry was responsible for supervising large numbers of people, some directly and some indirectly. He was also responsible for a large budget. At work, when he spoke, people listened. He carried great responsibility and great authority. This same power and authority that had initially attracted me to him soon made me feel smothered, controlled and micro-managed. You can begin to get a glimpse of the enormity of our differences.

When entering into marriage, both partners have their own strengths and weaknesses. **Sometimes the strengths can actually become curses instead of blessings if we don't submit our own wills and desires to God in our relationships.** Both partners bring baggage into a marriage. This baggage can separate the two from each other and hinder them from becoming one.

Most of us want to be married naturally, not supernaturally. In the end, what keeps us together is what is inside our hearts and our love for the Lord, not our love for ourselves. God is calling couples to learn to walk in agreement heart to heart, not head to head.

When Harry and I began to experience the normal challenges of marriage, I asked the Lord to teach me more about how to be married His way. I began to study what the Word says about marriage, asking for new revelation, new insight. The more I studied and reached out to God, the more He revealed to me. I've studied the Word for over thirty years, but these are revelations I have just received. He uncovered new layers of His truth for me to see. I think it was because I was at the end of myself and ready for Him to show me His way. My way was failing miserably.

When God created us as men and women out of what was previously a unified being, He gave us a choice to live together as one. As we have seen, before God separated man and woman during the creation process, man and woman lived together in a wonderful union close to the very heart of God and intimately close to each other.

Now we discover that man and woman were created to be uniquely different, like the left and right sides of the body. Yet they are to complete each other, not compete with each other. The power of relationship lies not in design, but in choice. It is in the choice to walk in agreement for a divine purpose that we discover the true purpose of marriage. After we were separated from God, and then from each other, we had to make the choice to return to the paradise of living close to God. We were also given the choice to live as one, united together in flesh as male and female.

*The truth is that we cannot live happily in a godly marriage when we use worldly principals of morality to make the marriage work.*

Scripture is full of information on this miraculous union called marriage. But somehow using the Bible as a reference Book on how to have a good marriage hasn't occurred to many people. We tend to go to self-help books; we listen to love songs on the radio about unrealistic relationships or, worse, failed relationships; we watch movies and read romance novels that create an illusion of fantasy and make a mockery of what true love between a man and a woman should be. These types of reference points have left us with an out-of-control divorce rate and thousands of unhappy, disillusioned men and women with no hope of ever finding the true longing of their hearts.

The truth is that we cannot live happily in a godly marriage when we use worldly principals of morality to make the marriage work. We wouldn't refer to a Ford manual to learn how a BMW works!

God ordained that men and women should be together and give comfort, support and love to each other. He said, *"It is not good for Man to be alone."* We discussed this earlier, but let's take a deeper look. In *Strong's Concordance,*[3] the definition of *alone* has several meanings. Two of these are the phrases *chief of his own city* and *of each alike.*

In Scripture, God did not place all the references to marriage in one convenient place. We are to work to receive His knowledge, like connecting the pieces of a puzzle. All the pieces are in the box, but we must continue to look, observe, twist and turn the pieces until they finally make a beautiful picture. God does not disclose deep scriptural teachings to people who do not diligently seek Him.

Truth is revealed to us a layer at a time, one piece at a time, with every Scripture we uncover. It is much like the way an archeologist carefully brushes off layer after layer of dirt and grime to uncover a buried treasure. When we have understood and benefited from the first layer, He gives us the next layer. These secrets I am about to share are valuable treasures that have been uncovered by meticulous study, meditation and revelation. They are written in the ancient Hebrew language and are often hidden from modern man's eyes. They can be found in the Talmud.

We were traveling a few years ago, speaking in the Chicago area. On one of our free afternoons, we went to a museum to view the Dead Sea Scrolls that were on display. The first thing I noticed was that there were three different Hebrew alphabets. In other words, the Hebrew alphabet has evolved in the appearance of the letters. I had been studying this very thing for a few years at this time. I discovered that the alphabet that I had been studying was the original one, the beginning alphabet of the ancient Hebrew language. It's just like God to do that for me. He knows that I like to know the beginnings of things. Everything grows out from the root!

Not only are there three evolutions of the language, but in this ancient Hebrew, every letter had three distinct dimensions. Each letter represents a sound, which is identified with a word or phrase. It also had a numerical value. For instance, the *alef,* our *A,* also represents the numerical value of one (1). It also has a definition told by a story, or an associated word. So each symbol has three distinct components: an alphabetical sound, a numerical value and a word or phrase of definition.

It's unfamiliar for us to think about language in these terms. But hidden within this ancient language are God's guiding principles for a happy marriage. The English translation does not reveal the nuances of meaning found in the original Hebrew language.

**In the Bible, God speaks frequently of unity.** In English, we have a broad understanding of what the word means. In Hebrew, the interpretation is more complex. The word "unity" means *one.* But when God speaks of walking in unity, He transcends our English meaning of merely being together. He says we are to become one flesh. This is a process that reveals the purifying fire of God that melts two people into one flesh in His sight.

## The Power of Agreement

God is giving us the opportunity to go back to the original state of humanity, the state of Adam in the garden before the division of male and female. Originally, mankind was one by design, male and female in one flesh, one body. But this reuniting is not by design; it's by choice. The true power of this kind of unity is attained by our own choosing.

When God talks about unity in the Church, He expects us all, no matter the number of people, to become one. The early Church walked in such unity that they shared all things in common. When one person hurt, the others felt it. When one person prospered, they all prospered. This was a totally unselfish way of living. It was never about the one person, but always about the whole body. This is God's kind of unity. His definition of unity is always about others in our lives. It is never a selfish mentality that is all about me!

In Hebrew, there are three symbols for the word *unity*:[4]

*This is what the ancient Hebrew symbols look like. The Hebrew alphabet has evolved over the years and current symbols may differ.*

The definition, "strongly fence the door," is not what we expect from the word *unity*.

That definition does not seem to fit what we think *unity* means. I couldn't help but wonder what that definition has to do with unity! *Strongly fence the door!* But when we take a deeper look, a defining moment begins to take shape for us.

These three symbols forming the word *unity* have a story of explanation with them. The story goes like this: Imagine all of us in a room together. I'm there, Harry is there. You are there. Your mate is there. Maybe many other people are there, too. Suddenly, a fire breaks out in the middle of this room. What would our instincts tell us to do? What is our initial response when it comes to fire? Run! Without a thought we would each draw quickly away, turn and try to find an exit! We would swiftly stampede to the nearest door. It's called self-preservation. It is a natural response to fire.

But what would happen if we reached the door, and all exits were barred, fenced, locked, with no way out? It may not be an easy answer, but it is a very simple truth. We would have to find a way to put out the fire. When we find ourselves with no escape and nowhere to run, we find a way to make it, to survive, to overcome, to put out the fire.

When fire breaks out in our lives, masked with the face of trouble, trials, circumstances, situations and problems, God's way is not to run away, but rather to find a way to put out the fire. Remember, the word *unity* means to "strongly fence the door." When we act and react in unity with our mate, we can find a way through the fire, trials, troubles and adversities of life, eventually emerging without even smelling of smoke like the three Hebrew children in the Book of Daniel.

In the movie *Apollo 13*, the flight crew was stranded in space with no way for their spacecraft to return to earth. The Mission Control Manager told the engineers and flight staff to come into the conference room and bring every piece of equipment to re-create an exact replica of the disabled space-craft. After everyone was gathered in the room, he locked the door and said, "No one is leaving this room until we find a way to get our crew home. Failure is not an option!" He "strongly fenced the door." In the end, a creative way was found to save the crew and the spacecraft! It was not easy, but it was possible with much effort on everyone's part to operate, think and move as one body.

Make a no-option plan to stay in your marriage! Search out the way to get oxygen from where you are right now to where God wants you to be, together and united. Married couples need to learn to "strongly fence the door" by acting in unity to protect each other, and to protect the union that God has joined together. Sometimes a mother-in-law can come to a home and complain that the house is a mess or that the children don't behave. Sometimes other people don't even realize what they are doing to bring division. No one will fight for and protect your union but you.

Each person in the marriage can approach his or her family before instances like this occur and tell them, "We are one. When you treat my mate badly, you treat me badly." Then tell them the things that are off limits to talk about. "Strongly fencing the door" and setting a few boundaries can make life run more smoothly; it's scriptural, and we can do it in love.

Another example of unity is found in the movie *We Were Soldiers*. General Moore, played by Mel Gibson, was facing a huge obstacle. The enemy had completely surrounded his men. They had run out of water to cool their mortar tubes and the enemy was threatening to break through their lines. General Moore immediately saw a solution. He stepped forward and began to urinate on the mortar tube. All the other men followed him and they produced enough liquid to cool down the mortar tube so they could fire again. This sounds unpleasant, but it's a great example of how men acting in one accord solved their problem. Individually, nobody possessed the means to alleviate the problem, but when everyone in unity did their part, the need was fully met.

Unity was also a major issue in the construction of the Tower of Babel, described in Genesis chapter eleven. The men and women of that time did not have the skills or architectural tools to build such a great tower, yet they achieved the impossible. In Genesis 11:6-7, we see that God the Father, Jesus and the Holy Spirit were all on the scene. They watched while spiritually ignorant men of that day attempted to build a towering monument to themselves. Pride was the true issue. Pride always has been the issue to divide, to conquer, to bring down and to destroy.

> *And they said, Come, let us build us a city and a tower whose top reaches into the sky, and let us make a name for ourselves, lest we be scattered over the whole earth.*
> Genesis 11:4, AMP

God knew that man wanted to use the power of unity in a way that would make him be like a god. Once again, pride was driving their actions. God understood better than anyone the power of unity in bringing results. Because of this, He confused their language. He divided the workers so they couldn't communicate with each other to finish this destructive, prideful project. This is what the enemy tries to do in each and every marriage. He tries to confuse the languages so that the male and the female feel like they are speaking a totally and completely different language from their partner. This is not God's plan. This is the plan of the enemy. We must recognize this evil plot against the plan of God in our marriages and families. **We must learn to run to God to unify us and teach us how to understand each other and speak the same language.**

# The Power of Agreement

Never forget this: "God finishes what He starts." What He divided at the tower of Babel, He finished on the Day of Pentecost in the second chapter of Acts. The Bible says that the believers were all in *"one accord."* When the Holy Spirit was given to the earth, the people actually understood each other in their different languages! This is what God wants us to do in our relationships. We are to rely on the Holy Spirit to show us, teach us and translate the language of our mates for us, so we can understand one another. Each marriage must have its own "Day of Pentecost" experience, in which God makes a way for us to speak His language of love so that we can finally communicate with and understand each other! When there are problems in this area, it is not really a breakdown in communication. It is not even a male/female difficulty. It is a division produced by the enemy to try to confuse us, breaking down our ability to build God's house within us. It is further magnified when we do not pray and seek God's help by the Spirit to help our weaknesses when understanding one another.

*We are to rely on the Holy Spirit to show us, teach us and translate the language of our mates for us, so we can understand one another.*

In this account in Genesis 11, we see that the Godhead, the Trinity, came to the scene without delay when the principle of unity was present. God's principles can be used for good or bad, and these men had made the choice of pride – the wrong choice! As individuals, they were incapable of building this tower; but when they were in unity, the project was no longer impossible. Everyone involved was doing what he or she could do, and that made the impossible possible. Unity is a very powerful concept. We have it available, right at our fingertips! When we act in unity, God comes on the scene. We don't have to beg or plead. He is right there. We read Christ's words in the Book of Matthew:

> *Again I tell you, if two of you on earth agree (harmonize together, make a symphony together) about whatever [anything and everything] they may ask, it will come to pass and be done for them by My Father in heaven.*
>
> Matthew 18:19, AMP

Harmony simply means coming into agreement, being on the same wavelength. The pitches can be varied. Some can be higher; others can be lower; but the blend of these sounds can truly be a harmonic symphony to God's ears! The Lord is eager to be where there is harmony. He refuses to be where there is quarreling and disagreement. Unity involves placing the needs and desires of others before our own. Unity is for the good of all, not for the benefit of just one. Unity and agreement can be attained by simply following the directions of these simple verses:

> *If you've gotten anything at all out of following Christ, if his love has made any difference in your life, if being in a community of the Spirit means anything to you, if you have a heart, if you care— then do me a favor: Agree with each other, love each other, be deep-spirited friends. Don't push your way to the front; don't sweet-talk your way to the top. Put yourself aside, and*

*help others get ahead. Don't be obsessed with getting your own advantage. Forget yourselves long enough to lend a helping hand.*

*Think of yourselves the way Christ Jesus thought of himself. He had equal status with God but didn't think so much of himself that he had to cling to the advantages of that status no matter what. Not at all. When the time came, he set aside the privileges of deity and took on the status of a slave, became human! Having become human, he stayed human. It was an incredibly humbling process. He didn't claim special privileges. Instead, he lived a selfless, obedient life and then died a selfless, obedient death—and the worst kind of death at that: a crucifixion.*

*Because of that obedience, God lifted him high and honored him far beyond anyone or anything, ever, so that all created beings in heaven and on earth – even those long ago dead and buried – will bow in worship before this Jesus Christ, and call out in praise that he is the Master of all, to the glorious honor of God the Father.*

Philippians 2:1-11, MSG

I believe this passage of Scripture sums up the concept of unity. It's not about just me. As long as we make it all about ourselves, we can neither be one with God nor with our mates. In fact, as long as our lives are wrapped up in our needs, our desires and what we can gain, unity is impossible to attain.

Remember my little phrase? "It is not worth it to be right."

Insisting upon being right can cost you more than you are willing to pay. Being right can cost you every relationship on earth. Nothing is worth that!

# 2 BECOMING 1

Most likely, if we entered a room where people were arguing, we would turn around and leave as quickly as possible. Well, guess what? God doesn't like arguing, either. He definitely won't stick around for that! When we cannot agree, it's useless to look for God. He won't be there. When we can find a way to agree, God promises always to be there.

Agreement gets God on the scene. Agreement in God's sight is like a legal summons to the throne room! If we want Him to come into our lives and help us with our problems, we need to search for a way to come into agreement with one another.

Harry laughs and says, "When Cheryl and I are not in sync, I take her by the hand, lead her outside and ask her if we can at least agree that the sky is blue." It sounds funny and oversimplified, but have you ever tried it? **The next time you find yourself in discord with your mate, make it a point to be the first to soften, to smile, to give in.** Make it a point to agree. Watch how quickly the mood changes! It's a God thing.

Some couples say, "Well, we just can't agree on anything." If that's true for you, then find some neutral ground somewhere and start there! Learn to agree on simple things at first. As I mentioned before, agreeing that the grass is green and the sky is blue is a good place to start. When we really search for things on which we can agree, it gets easier. We can build agreement on simple things before we tackle the areas on which we disagree. Until we learn how to give in on certain issues, it is better to avoid those when possible. Avoiding is not the answer forever. It is just an intermediary place until the gradual process of coming into agreement can be attained. Agreement is not easy. If it were easy, then everyone would do it. Agreement is hard work. And it is continuous. There is always another opportunity to agree or disagree!

Remember the phrase I referred to previously? I finally learned it after years of being married and not having a clue how to agree and walk as one with my husband. "It's not worth it to be right." When we are trying to attain unity, we all need to learn when not to make our point!

Harry says there are two words that can be a key to a happy marriage, "Yes, dear." I say that two more words are, "Give in." We all need to find our own two words and rehearse them regularly.

When I was younger, I felt every thought that I had was a revelation and just had to be said! Now as I am maturing, I find myself in all situations asking God, "Do You want

me to say that?" There are times when just being quiet is the best choice.

*Be still, and know that I am God...*

Psalm 46:10, KJV

## Chapter Eight

# GOD'S PURIFYING FIRE

~

### *Harry and Cheryl*

We have worked hard in this area of agreement. Guess what? We will always have to work at it, because it is not natural for human beings to submit to one another. Our natural instinct is to take care of ourselves. We automatically default to looking out for number one! But walking in agreement means continually putting ourselves aside and looking out for the needs and desires of others.

Remember the tire tool story? That was like the last straw, the last place for me to finally get it! I just could not seem to understand why God would want me to agree with my mate when he was so obviously wrong! But it wasn't about being right or wrong. It was about unity, agreement, and walking and operating in a position that invites God into our lives, our homes and our hearts as one.

# 2 BECOMING 1

More revelation about marriage comes when we study the Hebrew word for *male,* which is similar to the word for *husband.* The word *female* is similar to the word for *wife* in the ancient Hebrew language.[5]

(Male/Husband = *Strong's* # 376)  W ↲ Ӑ

(Female/Wife = *Strong's* # 802)   �氙 W Ӑ

(Fire = *Strong's* # 784)  W Ӑ

The word *husband* or *male* in Hebrew has three symbols.

Remember, in Hebrew writings the letters and the words read right to left, not left to right as our English language.

The definition of these three symbols when they are put together mean, *"His hand is in the midst of the fire."*[6] We must remember that each individual symbol has a definition. Then the combination of the symbols gives us the story for each word.

These three symbols each have distinct meaning as they stand alone.

The first symbol means *strong* or leader. Ӑ

The middle symbol means *hand.* ↲

The third symbol means *devourer.* W

What you must realize as you study this is that the first and last symbols combined mean *strong devourer (fire).* W Ӑ

*Read right to left.*

When we studied the word *fire* in the *Strong's Concordance,* we found that it looks and even sounds very close to the word, *male.* That's because two-thirds of male is fire!

Now when you understand the parts, the whole begins to make sense. "His hand is in the midst of the fire." The symbol for hand is in the middle of the two symbols for fire; thus, his hand is in the midst (or middle) of the fire.

Remember that in Hebrews the Word says, *"For our God [is indeed] a consuming fire"* (Hebrews 12:29, AMP). **The male is to keep his hand in the midst of God. He is to stay connected to the Father at all times.** The male is designed by God to be the divine connection to God.

The three symbols that combine to form the words for *female/wife* are, *What comes out of.* It's easy to see where this definition comes from when you consider that the female is taken out of mankind, leaving the male (half of God's image). But woman was not taken out of just any part of man; rather, she came out of the fire of man. The God part of the male helps to produce the female side of God's image on this earth.

Let's take the three symbols apart here and look at each one individually:

The first symbol, which means *strong,* and the second symbol, which means *devourer,* spell *fire.*

The third symbol for *wife/female* is completely different from the three symbols for *male.* When this symbol is put at the end of a word, it means *what comes out of.*

When you study the three symbols for *male* and *female* side by side, you see that two of the symbols for *male/husband* are the same as two of the symbols for *female/wife.* These two symbols mean *strong* and *devourer.* Together they

135

mean, *fire,* which is easy to understand since we still view fire today as a *strong devourer.*

## *Male*

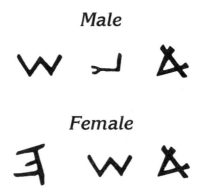

## *Female*

"What comes out of the fire," is the only dissimilar symbol for the female. *"His hand"* is the only dissimilar symbol for the male. There are definitely differences between male and female, and they seem to be much deeper than just two little Hebrew symbols. But are they deeper? Is this what makes it so hard to agree, to see things from each other's point of view? Is this why we always seem to be coming from different perspectives with different sides of the story? Is this why one seems to be so predominantly left and the other so predominantly right? Opposites?

It would seem that these two small differences birth the unhappiness, discord, disharmony, disagreement, bitterness and anger in our relationships. Or is that the case? When we take these two different symbols and place them together, we find that they actually spell an ancient Hebrew word.[vii]

## *Male*

## *Female*

The difference between the words for *male* and *female* spell the word *Yah*.

**When you put these two symbols together they spell *Yah*, which translates to, "the Lord in the land of the living."** Quite simply, when you take the difference between the symbols for *male* and *female* and you place them together in agreement, it spells *God ... the Lord in the land of the living!* I don't know about you, but this is shout-worthy news to me!

Can you see why evil forces work so hard to keep us divided? Can you see why anything and everything can try to come between us and keep us from getting over ourselves enough to see the whole, big picture put together instead of just seeing the two parts? Our division is what keeps God out of our marriages and our homes. Our agreement is what brings God, the Lord in the land of the living, into our marriages and our homes!

It is in the total and complete surrender of our own wills and desires that we bring God onto the scene of our lives, our homes, our marriages. It is in the dying of two that the One can be birthed in our relationships.

Now the revelation makes so much more sense. We were created in one body, and God said that it is not good that man should be alone. That word *alone* in the *Strong's Concordance* is represented by numbers 909 and 905. In other words, it is not good that man should be *chief of his city*. Another rendering would be that it is not good that man should be *of each alike, unable to reproduce.*

I believe these two definitions show that man was originally made both male and female. We know this from Genesis 5:2 where it says, *"He created them male and female and blessed them and named them [both] Adam [Man] at the time they were created."*

In the beginning we were created as one species, but also in one body. When God said that it is not good that man should be *of each alike*, both male and female in one body (Genesis 2:18), He made a plan to separate the species of mankind into two genders. No longer one by design, now oneness could only be attained by choice. Therein lies the power of agreement, the power of reproduction, that brings God on the scene: our own choice!

Then we find that after God says, *"it is not good ..."* He further says, *"..I will make him a helpmeet..."* This word, *helpmeet*, has an incredible definition when using the *Strong's Concordance*. There are two different numbers representing the word *helpmeet*: #5828 and #5048. Here are just a few of the meanings: "Help," meaning *aid*; "meet," meaning *a front, a part opposite, specifically, a counterpart, or mate, usually (over, against, or before)*. This is my favorite part. I think it's the most enlightening: *his other side, his other sight, his other view.*

When you stop and think about this, you can easily see the true meaning. Mankind was originally created male and female as one; in other words, in one body. God said that the design was wonderful, but there was no power in it. The earth is all about choice. My sole purpose for being here is to choose, to make a choice to love God and to be one with Him...or not to choose Him. This is my choice. God will not make it for me. He wants me to be in Him because I choose to be, not because I have to as a result of being designed that way.

This also applies to our relationships. When male and female were one by design, there was no power in that union. There was no choice to be made to walk as one. Male and female were not given the power of choice. Thus, we were not and could not fulfill what God said about mankind:

> God said, Let Us [Father, Son, and Holy Spirit] make mankind in Our image, after Our likeness, and let them have complete authority over the fish of the sea, the birds of the air, the [tame] beasts, and over all of the earth, and over everything that creeps upon the earth. So God created man in His own image, in the image and likeness of God He created him; male and female He created them.
>
> Genesis 1:26-27, AMP

To be in the true image of the Godhead, we had to operate as one, but be separate, just like the Father, Son and the Holy Spirit. This is the design: We were created as one, then separated with the choice to come together and operate as one!

## SEPARATE by design
## + ONE by choice
## POWER

From the definitions of the Hebraic symbols, we can see that the uniqueness of male and female are parts that make up the whole of the image of God. It is not that one side is smarter, more important or more useful than the other. On the contrary, it is only in the blending of the two parts, the two sides, the two views, the two sights that we have the whole, complete image of God.

Now you might be thinking, "But how can a triune Being, Who is Father, Son and Holy Spirit, make mankind in Their image, and their image is only two, male and female? Where is the triune? Why are there only two?" A mirror reflection, which is called an image, is the exact likeness of what is being reflected. The only way this image is not the same is if the mirror is distorted. Perhaps that is why many relationships do not look like God. They are a distorted image of Him. A true mirror is not a trick mirror.

**Isolation and solitude are both enemies of unity.** They deceive and distort God's image. But it is within our own ability to reflect God's image in a true and undistorted way. This is accomplished by truth, with no deception, no lies, nothing hidden and nothing missing in our relationships. We have the ability to correctly reflect God's image through our unity, but many couples still reflect a distorted image. Why?

Do you remember that when we took the differences in the two words with the three symbols for male and female and put them together, they spelled "*Yah, the Lord in the land of the living*"? One of the dimensions of God is represented in our reflection of Him on the earth. We reflect *Yah, the Lord in the land of the living.* Is your marriage alive? Or is it a dead marriage? When we have truly submitted our wills, our lives and our relationship to the will and purpose of God for our lives together, our marriages become supernaturally alive!

Here is the key. When male and female are not walking in agreement, they are not reflecting God's image. It is only when we come together by our choice to walk in agreement, no matter the circumstances, that God is in the midst of our relationship. This act of agreement not only brings God onto the scene of our lives, but it actually makes us reflect the image in which we were created.

No longer are we two being one; by the choice of getting over ourselves enough to come together, we reflect the image of the Three in One, the Triune Godhead.

Father *(male)*

Son *(Jesus, the Lord in the land of the living — Yah)*

Holy Spirit *Helper/Comforter/female)*

Thus, triune image reflects Triune image!

The Godhead is vertically Triune.

The marriage relationship in agreement has Jesus in it (Matthew 18), causing two to become three (triune).

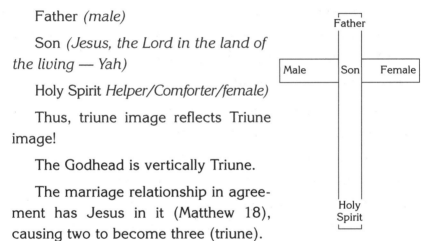

Now meditate and think on this ...*selah* ... pause and calmly think of that!

Agreement takes us to the cross in our relationship. Without Jesus in the midst of us, in our own ability we cannot accomplish the true triune image of God. With Jesus in our relationships (male, Jesus, female), we are triune.

Please don't misunderstand here. I do not mean to say that the Holy Spirit is female. We know that in the spiritual realm, there is neither male nor female. There is no reason for reproduction. The reference here of assigning male to Father and female to Holy Spirit is merely so that the mirror-reflected image of Who God has made us can be better understood by our finite mental capacities.

There was never a creation of the female; but the Bible says that once she was taken out of man, then God formed her. She could not be created again, because she was already created in Genesis 1:26-27.

In Genesis chapter two, when God put man to sleep and took a rib out of the male to form the female, He reached into the fire of man and separated the one side from the other. The symbolism of the rib, or side, of man represents the definition in the *Strong's: "his other sight, his other view, his other side."*

This is the beginning of the two having the choice to become one flesh. Let's not forget this is a great example for us to remember of what Jesus did for us on the cross of Calvary. The last place that He was pierced was in His side. The fifth cut of covenant was to make entrance possible back into Oneness with Him. This signifies that the bride of Christ can be reunited in the side wound of the Bridegroom, side by side. The bride of Christ – the ready and waiting, prepared and purified church – has the opportunity to be reunited in agreement with our soon coming King, our Bridegroom. We came out of the side, and we reunite at the side! This cut had to be made so that we could enter back into right relationship by our own choice. God made the way. We make the choice.

The Book of John describes this as an engrafting of the branch to the tree or the vine (15:4-5). We are the branch and Jesus, our Bridegroom, is the Vine or Tree with which we have the privilege of becoming one for all of eternity!

# God's Purifying Fire

God put mankind, the male/female, asleep so that He could reach into man's side, where God's fire is, and take out or separate the female from the male. We must remember that the definition for female is "what comes out of the fire."

God did not simply remove a rib from the male. If it had been as simple as that, then the male's anatomy would possess one fewer rib than the female's. God took out the "other side, the other sight, the other view." He pulled apart the male and female to correspond with all other living creation. There had to be the seed giver and the seed receiver; the life giver and the life receiver to complete the image of God on the earth. **Our God is the Life Giver. We are the life receiver.**

*When we agree together in unity, we look more like God than anything else on the face of the earth.*

Thus, the whole man became two parts, male and female. The power and image of God could only be attained once again by choice. God has given us the power to choose; in

this choice lies the very power to be in His image while we still live here on this earth.

This is not easy, but it truly is simple. We must die to our own desires, our own thoughts, our own ways, to become what we were ultimately created to be: His image!

He created one half male and the other half female in His likeness and image. That means that God has both the attributes of the male and the female. He is both logical and illogical. He is cerebral, physical, emotional. He is soft and nurturing as well as strong and disciplining. He is all in all.

## 2 BECOMING 1

God is Spirit. Since we were created to be like Him, we are spirit, too. When we agree together in unity, we look more like God than anything else on the face of the earth. And we have the power of God activated in our lives; two becoming three in one (male, Jesus, female)!

This really frightens the mortal and marital enemy, Satan. In marriage, when we come together without disagreement, anger or divorce, we are walking in unity, God's plan for every godly relationship. That's why Satan does everything he can to keep us separated. When we are in agreement, we have God's kind of power on this earth to take the impossible and make it possible.

When God is in the center of our marriages, we are literally making Him God in the land of our living relationship.

When we do not have God in the center of our marriages, we feel as though our union is dead; and so it is, whenever the Lord is not invited inside. Many people actually refer to their marriage as a dead marriage. When God is not in our relationship, when we have not found the way to walk as one in our marriage, then it is dead where it stands.

Jesus said:

*Again I tell you, if two of you on earth agree (harmonize together, make a symphony together) about whatever [anything and everything] they may ask, it will come to pass and be done for them by My Father in heaven. For wherever two or three are gathered (drawn together as My followers) in (into) My name, there I AM in the midst of them.*

Matthew 18:19-20, AMP

Jesus is in the midst of them. It is so true, and it packs double the power when we can live this way in our marriages!

In the Hebrew language, the words *strong devourer* or *fire* are a type of fire that is the strongest devourer on the face of the earth. When you take God out of your marriage, all you have left is the most destructive force on earth. It is a consuming, destructive, devouring fire. There is not just one fire, but two raging fires combined, without the power of God to make them a purifying fire!

*Male*        *Female*

### Fire of Fire

Any word in the ancient Hebrew language that is doubled means that it is the greatest, the biggest, the most powerful, the highest, the worst kind, the most devastating...it is the superlative of its meaning. Some examples are phrases such as King of kings, Lord of lords, Holy of Holies, or fire of fire (the destruction of relationships forever).

*Male*        *Female*

### Fire of Fire

It is interesting that in the Hebrew there are two kinds of fire.[8] One is the *Fire of the Prince,* which is God's kind of fire. This kind of fire is rooted in humility. We see this when we put ourselves aside long enough to let others get ahead (see Philippians 2, MSG). This kind of fire produces life, the way and the truth. This kind of fire in our relationships blesses, leads straight and brings about joy and happiness. Purity, holiness and righteousness are always birthed out of God's kind of fire.

When a husband is operating in this kind of fire, his own life has the opportunity to be purified, his wife's life has the opportunity to be purified, his children's lives have the opportunity to be purified and all relationships in every direction have this same opportunity. When the husband is operating in the Fire of the Prince, not only is he going to be the godly man that he was created to be, with his life being constantly purified and tried by fire; but he will give the opportunity for purification to his wife as well because she comes out of his fire. With the man's hand in God's fire, then his fire, his life, will always produce the best outcome with all of his relationships.

"It's all about others," says the Fire of the Prince.

The other kind of fire is the *Fire of Chaos*.[9] When we don't operate in the Fire of the Prince, then we operate in the Fire of Chaos. There is no other neutral ground. Every person is either operating in one or the other type of fire. Two thirds of every human being is fire. What kind of fire are you? What are you producing for others to see?

The Fire of Chaos is the exact opposite of the Fire of the Prince. Every question word, such as who, what, where, when, why and how much, has one common symbol in Hebrew. It is the symbol for chaos.

When we get hung up in questions that begin with any of these words, we are opening the door for the Fire of Chaos to begin to burn in our lives. The Fire of Chaos is rooted in pride. "It's all about me," says this fire.

Do any of these questions sound familiar?

"Why did God give me this mate?"

"Why do I have to go through this?"

"When is God going to show up on the scene and change this woman?"

"What did I do to deserve such a man?"

"Why is she always taking the opposite view from me?"

On and on these questions go. The more we ask them, the more deeply we become entangled in the deception! It is a vicious cycle that can only be broken by choice. We must choose to stop the vicious cycle of asking questions with no answers. We must choose to put ourselves aside, no longer two by design, but one by choice! It's time we stop being who we want to be and become who God created us to be!

Chaos is always rooted in pride. It asserts itself, bringing confusion and strife by insisting, "I am more important than anybody else!" When that happens, we literally bring the Fire of Destruction down on our lives, on our marriages, on our homes and on our relationship with Jesus. Our children will be birthed out of chaos instead of the Prince. Without God's purifying fire, things not only stay the same, they get worse! Life is like a domino effect: God's presence in our lives creates hope, a future and good things, whereas lack of relationship with Him brings waves of despair, shame and destruction.

Now we can see why the power of agreement is the most important force on the earth today. God's Word tells us to get into agreement with one another, to put ourselves aside, and to allow our mate to be elevated. When our mate shines, we shine. Both are being elevated, both are being lifted up, each by the other in true humility. Now we're both where we need to be and we get there in God's way.

Many have settled for a worldly kind of marriage, a fake marriage. Only in God and with God can marriage prosper, becoming all that it was meant to be. God wants us to have a marriage that will give true happiness to both partners.

There's a story about a young girl who had a strand of fake pearls that she loved to wear. One day her father asked her if she loved her pearls more than she loved him.

"Would you give me your pearls?" he asked. The girl squirmed, but couldn't release the beloved pearls. She tossed and turned that night, unable to sleep. In the morning, she crept into her parent's bedroom with the pearls clutched in her hand. She proudly told her father, "I want you to have these because you are more important to me than my pearls."

Her father quickly got out of bed and went to his briefcase. "I'm glad you feel that way. On my recent trip I got you a strand of real pearls. You don't have to wear the fake pearls anymore."

Isn't it wonderful to have the real thing? How much better is a true union with our mate than enduring a hollow, artificial marriage, as promoted by the world?

The choice is yours.

# My Prayer of Commitment

*Dear Lord,*

*I give my life to You. I give You my past, present and future. I want to first be one with You so that who I was no longer exists. I want only a future with You, my Lord, my Savior, Jesus Christ. I commit to follow You all the days of my life.*

*I give You my mate. I give You our marriage and our union. I trust You to do what You need to do in my life and in my mate's life for us to truly become one in Your way. Help me to get over myself. Teach me to focus on the needs of my mate and not only on my own needs. Make us one, Father. We take up a no-option plan to see this marriage through to victory. We commit our future into Your Hands.*

_____          _____

*(Husband's Signature)*          *(Wife's Signature)*

# ABOUT THE AUTHORS

*H*arry and Cheryl Salem have a beautiful love story to tell. It began in 1985, when a confident, successful businessman met Miss America. Sparks instantly flew! They soon wed, but the honeymoon stage didn't last forever. Through desperate, low valleys and tremendous high places, this couple has walked—not always in perfect harmony, but still together and in agreement. They have tapped into a vital key for a successful, solid, and happy relationship: Agreement.

May this story of love, trust and learning to put God first in all things inspire you in your relationships, vertically with God as well as horizontally with others.

*Salem Family Ministries* focuses on family and restoration. The Salems stress the unity of family, marriage, personal relationships, financial goals and parenting. They also lead motivational meetings and men's and ladies' conferences on the subjects of overcoming obstacles such as abuse, abandonment, poor self-image and financial difficulty.

Together, Harry and Cheryl have written over 23 books, including *An Angel's Touch* (a top-25 best-seller), *Distractions from Destiny, From Grief to Glory* and *From Mourning to Morning*.

The Salems' ministry is based in Tulsa, Oklahoma. Harry and Cheryl have two sons, Harry III and Roman, and a beautiful daughter, Gabrielle, who lives in Heaven.

## TO CONTACT HARRY AND CHERYL SALEM:

Salem Family Ministries
P.O. Box 701287, Tulsa, OK 74170
918.369.8008
*www.salemfamilyministries.org*

Please include your prayer requests and comments when you write.

# OTHER BOOKS BY
# HARRY AND CHERYL SALEM

*The Choice Is Yours*

*40 Day Prayer Journal – Overcoming Fear*

*Every Body Needs Balance*

*From Grief to Glory*

*Distractions from Destiny*

*From Mourning to Morning*

*Speak the Word over Your Family for Finances*

*Speak the Word over Your Family for Healing*

*Speak the Word over Your Family for Salvation*

*Covenant Conquerors*

*Warriors of the Word*

*Fight in the Heavenlies* (out of print)

*It's Too Soon to Give Up*

*Being #1 at Being #2*

*For Men Only*

*An Angel's Touch*

*A Royal Child*

*The Mommy Book*

*How to Get a Balanced Body* (out of print)

*Simple Facts about Salvation, Healing & the Holy Ghost*
(out of print)

*Health & Beauty Secrets* (out of print)

*Choose to be Happy* (out of print)

*Abuse...Bruised but Not Broken*

*You Are Somebody*

*A Bright Shining Place — The Story of a Miracle*

# ENDNOTES

1. *www.mcn.org/rop/rop/mitch/mm*

2. *www.smithsonianmag.si.edu/smithsonian/issues04/ mar04/phenomena.html*. It is important to note here that of this research, we only used that information which we found to be documented scientific fact. We are not endorsing these authors or any of their writings found in these articles or any other articles in any way.

3. Strong, James, *Abingdon's Strong's Exhaustive Concordance of the Bible* (Nashville: Abingdon, 1980).

4. Here we have been very influenced by the work of Frank T. Seekins. See his *Hebrew Word Pictures* (Phoenix: Living Word Pictures, Inc., 1994). *www.livingwordpictures.com* Used with permission.

5. Please note that the drawings in these chapters depict what the ancient Hebrew symbols looked like. The Hebrew alphabet has evolved over the years and current symbols may differ.

6. Seekins, *Hebrew Word Pictures*.

7. ibid.

8. ibid.

9. ibid.